D1261138

SCREWBALL

SCREWBALL

Tug McGraw

Joseph Durso

Houghton Mifflin Company Boston
1974

FIRST PRINTING V

Library of Congress Cataloging in Publication Data

McGraw, Tug, 1944–
Screwball.

1. McGraw, Tug. 1944–   2. Baseball.   3. New
York (City).   Baseball club (National League, Mets)
I. Durso, Joseph, joint author.   II. Title.
GV865.M312A37   796.357'092'4   74-2132
ISBN 0-395-18646-3

To Mom for bringing me in
To Dad and Hank for getting me going
And to Phyllis for putting it all together

—T.McG.

Contents

Illustrations

I would I might forget that I am I
And break the heavy chain that binds me fast
    Whose links about myself
    My deeds have cast.

                — *Santayana.*

1

The Magnificent Screwball

To THE FRENCH, especially the Canadians on the northern flank of the American sporting scene, it is called "la balle tire-bouchon" — the corkscrew ball. To the 600 players in the major leagues, many of whom swing at it with a thirty-three-ounce stick, it is "the screwjie" — or, depending on the geography and phonetics of the locker room, "the scroogie." To the public, which buys 30,000,000 seats every summer to watch it thrown a distance of sixty and a half feet: the screwball.

But whatever it's called, however it's spelled, wherever it's watched, most people agree that Frank Edwin Mc-Graw, Jr., of the New York Mets both throws — and probably *is* — the most magnificent screwball in modern professional sports.

A cool cat, the modern professional athlete. Man of distinction of the nineteen seventies. Comes lurching into your living room with briefcase, bonus, business manager, tax shelter, supersell, and Howard Cosell. He is overpaid and underworked, glorified, idolized, commercialized, beatified. Also patronized, publicized, pampered, laundered. The very model of a plastic model glittering across your TV screen, and he's got it made.

What follows is a look at one such modern professional athlete: Tug McGraw. This is a report on fear. Also joy, grief, pride, tension, panic. Anxiety, self-doubt, self-guilt, self-torture. A bundle of nerves to go with his bundle of brass, hang-ups to go with his change-ups, highs to match his lows. And any resemblance between the private him and the public cool cat above is unintentional, unrecognizable, and maybe unthinkable.

You watch Number 45 ride across your screen in that clever little bullpen go-cart shaped like a huge baseball cap. You see him leap out to rising applause and an Irish reel on the stadium organ and stretch on the slab of whitened rubber six inches wide and twenty-four inches long that is embedded in the mound of dirt at center stage. You see him wheel, deal, and whip one toward the five-sided target known as home plate, seventeen inches from front to farthest point back and twelve inches wide, and he does it all for something like $90,000 a summer.

The object is to throw the ball past the man standing there with the white-ash stick, a piece of solid wood that cannot extend more than forty-two inches from knob to barrel, where it cannot measure more than two and three-fourths inches around. The ball itself being, according to Paragraph 1.09 of the eighty-seven-page manual titled "Official Baseball Rules": "a sphere formed by yarn wound around a small core of cork, rubber or similar material, covered with two strips of white horsehide tightly stitched together, not less than five nor more than five and one-quarter ounces avoirdupois and not less than nine nor more than nine and one-quarter inches in circumference."

Or, whether Number 45 throws the ball past the plate or not, in the absolutely indisputable words of Casey Stengel, "It takes twenty-seven outs to win."

It may not be death in the afternoon, the moment of truth, the national pastime, or any of the clichés that surround and dramatize our leisure hours and their casts of characters. But it is fun and even fantasy, and the geometry hasn't changed much in a century and a half.

Inside the instant replay of Number 45's mind, though, what manner of man do we watch earning that $90,000 within the ninety-foot-square infield and the green yard that stretches another 300 feet beyond? Does he think, remember, recall, recoil, wonder, and struggle while he tries to stretch, wheel, deal, and whip it across? Does he beat his wife, love his parents, hate his boss, fear his work, educate his kids, fight his phantoms? Does he pay his taxes, pay the fiddler, pay the price?

I can tell you the public facts about McGraw in a hurry. Born August 30, 1944, in Martinez, California. Throws left-handed, bats right-handed. Raised in Vallejo, about twenty-five miles outside San Francisco; cut classes at St. Vincent's High School and Vallejo Junior College; signed first professional contract in 1964 and got a bonus of $7000, most of which he promptly spent on a convertible. Outpitched Sandy Koufax as a rookie, then didn't outpitch anybody in particular until he was made a relief pitcher in 1969. Married Phyllis Kline, a TWA stewardess, that year. Two children, lives near San Diego, works a continent away in New York, and he's the highest paid relief pitcher in baseball history.

Also the most emotional, and thereby hangs a tale. He sulks, he exults. He often flings his arms straight up into the air and sometimes falls flat on the ground. Intense, fresh-faced, hyperactive. And he has high highs, low lows, and one of the great screwballs of all time, a pitch that looks something like a fastball when it starts but then slants away from a right-handed batter, down and out, when it finishes.

He arrived in spring training one year with a mustache and a General Custer hairdo when the Mets had a rule against long hair: Gil Hodges made him shave the former and clip the latter. He arrived another year with fifteen extra pounds when they had a rule against weight, and Hodges made him lose that. He tried some dives off the high board another year when both the pool and the ocean were off-limits, and Hodges ordered him beached. In the bullpen at Shea Stadium, he helped cultivate tomatoes in the dirt and gnawed spareribs on the bench, and when he heard on a TV talk show that corn was ideal for muscle energy, he became a corn freak.

Once he got into a friendly argument with two small boys, Gary and Steven Lewbell, the sons of his friend and business confidant in New York. The issue was whether a pitcher could commit a balk if nobody was on base at the time. The boys said yes; McGraw said no. In fact, he persisted, "I could fall down or throw the ball into the stands as long as nobody was on base."

So the next day in the eighth inning of a game, he found nobody on base, glanced up into the stands, spotted his little friends, and decided to demonstrate his theory. He wound up and promptly fell down while in full pitching motion.

"Nothing happened," McGraw reported, flushed with success. "The umpire didn't call it a balk or anything."

"Of course," he conceded, with only a trace of embarrassment, "some people raised eyebrows — including the manager."

But when people began to suspect that he was either immature or flamboyant, he instructed his fan clubs to divert their time, trouble, and money to helping American Indians, and he suddenly started getting phone calls from the White House and the Ford Foundation.

He joined the marines, became a trained jungle fighter and killer, and decided that he hated violence. He compiled a reading list of books on Vietnam and national politics, then switched to Japanese poetry. He "didn't want to spend the winter driving a truck in California," so he created the Youth Encouragement Program of Vallejo. It had an office in his apartment, an emblem showing a young man astride a globe, and a list of local business sponsors like Scofield's Gas Station and Pluto's Hot Dogs, and he said its aim was to keep kids from dropping out of school or dropping out of sight.

He had a predilection for long hair, but still settled with convention long enough to become the team barber, a talent he had developed as a student on the back porch of his house across the street from the high school. Later, in the days before he developed a fancier talent as the team screwball specialist, he worried that he might need a sideline to make a living and attended the Tri-City school for barbers on the Bowery.

"I have a lifetime of being a showoff guy," he once conceded. "But that doesn't make me a bad guy. I was always exuberant and liked to have fun. I always was cocky. But so much of it was to hide my own insecurity."

To hide my own insecurity — is that the answer? Was it just the trauma of the runt of the litter who grew up alongside a big brother who hit home runs and parents who argued and hassled themselves into divorce? I don't know. I also don't know if Lee Trevino had to be penniless as a child in order to become a golf millionaire as an adult. Or whether Larry Csonka and Jim Kiick had to play football for demanding coaches in order to become jolly rebels as pros.

All I know is that McGraw has had more insecurity in his private life, and more security in his public life, than almost anybody else performing every day in the all-American fishbowl. And the chemistry of that strange equation — what it is in a man's private life that equals what he becomes in his public life — completes the portrait.

My portrait of McGraw started coming into focus toward the end of the baseball season one evening a few years ago. I was traveling with the Mets at the time, one year after they had stunned the human race by winning the World Series after seven years of stumbling through the wilderness. Men had walked on the moon that summer and, everything considered, it had been one hell of a year for extra effort. But now, twelve months later, the Mets were no longer king of the hill. And when I returned to the Pittsburgh Hilton Hotel from dinner after they had been eliminated from contention by the Pittsburgh Pirates, I found a note slipped under my door.

It was inside a hotel envelope with two words printed in blue ink across the top: "Hey Joe," with a pair of exclamation points. Then in two neatly printed lines beneath: "Funny your name should be Joe."

The message in the envelope was written in the same print-style, but in pencil, on five small memo-sized sheets from a liquor store pad.

Page one consisted only of the, what shall I say, historical facts: "Sat. 26 September 1970" (in three lines) and "7:50 P.M., Pitt. Penna." (in two lines). My first impression was that it was a prank by a drinking member of the formerly amazing Mets. It was no prank, but it *was* from a drinking member of the formerly amazing Mets, and a hurting one, at that. I was batting .500.

"My good, hopefully understanding friend Joe," it read. "I am at this writing, sitting and wanting to let the world know how I feel (the world being my most personal friend).

"For whatever reason, I (over a couple of beers and two Manhattans on the rocks) (not to mention the delimea (spelling?) of the past few weeks) was compelled (not knowing the full meaning of the word) to write this, my first poem. Respectfully, Tug — the Ballplayer."

Then came the poem in nine lines, with little circles, squares, dots, dashes, and ellipses after certain lines. According to a code supplied underneath, they were symbols for "thought," "thought — one kind," "thought — another kind," and "confusion — but thought." And the poem itself read:

> Four to three . . . . .
> It seems so terrible
> But . . . .
> It's not that bad.

God knows I tried
I swear I did my best.
He was better than me
This time . . . .
Thank you God, for tomorrow.

The next little page reverted to prose: "Dear Joe —
some afterthought verses — or separate poems." And
on the last sheet:

The death of an athlete . . . .
I've accomplished all
That I can accomplish . . . . . .
From that . . . .

Please bring that back,
I know I won't miss . . . .
Again . . . . this time . . .
Shit . . .

Well, what do you do about that? There were twenty-
five players on the Mets who had been bounced out of
the pennant race that afternoon by the Pirates, and
twenty-four of them had swallowed their pride, drowned
their sorrows, or hidden their chagrin without trying to
express things in poetry, let alone to the writer from the
New York *Times*.

One minute I'd been wary that the twenty-fifth
member of the company was putting me on or putting
me down; the next minute, though, I felt that he was actually groping for — for what? A shoulder to cry on? A
friend to lean on? Maybe McGraw had spilled those
beers and Manhattans with his roommate, maybe he had
telephoned home to get some sympathy, like everybody
else, after Hodges had called each man into his office and
assigned him a reporting weight for the following spring.

"The trouble with the Mets," one of their own staff officials said, putting it all into a perspective of sorts, "is that they still have last year's money in their pockets."

That was okay for the economics of their collapse. But unless I was misreading the seventeen lines written by McGraw, a twenty-five-year-old relief pitcher somehow composing his "first poem," some of them at least were still searching for answers. Every team that wins eventually loses, but here was one guy who went to a pretty far-fetched extreme to find phrases for *what* he had lost. Not many ballplayers sit down and write notes about it, and I didn't know whether to laugh, cry, call him up on the house phone, or just sit and wonder. I sat and wondered.

I also offered to give the note back to him when I saw him at the ball park the next afternoon. But McGraw said no, he'd just picked me out for some one-on-one rapping, and he hoped I didn't mind.

Since McGraw and I hadn't ever gotten far past the normal manners of any traveling entourage in pro sports, I wasn't quite sure how to carry it off. Ballplayers are usually closer to each other than any of them is to the manager, the four coaches, or the eight or ten writers and broadcasters who cross the country with them for six months every year.

Ballplayers come in all sizes and shapes and moods. An intellectual and loner like Jim McAndrew, a prim psychology graduate of the University of Iowa, a pitcher they call "Moms" in needling moments. Tom Seaver, proper, slightly pompous, so organized that he makes anybody else appear at loose ends, working the big crossword puzzle in the Sunday *Times* and analyzing his own performances in clinical detail. Rusty Staub, tall and red-haired and professional, the team bachelor with the look and bearing of Rhett Butler making $110,000 a season, and he can cook, too. Bud Harrelson, the midget shortstop, Seaver's down-to-earth roommate, mighty mouse in a Superman T-shirt. Willie Mays, chattering in a high squeal, totally his own man, sometimes sullen, sometimes soaring, a household god the younger guys both respect and slightly resent. And, in three locker cubicles at one end of the clubhouse, the coaches: Eddie Yost, antiseptic; Rube Walker, warm country bear; Joe Pignatano, the Chico Marx of the bullpen.

And McGraw. Not too short, maybe an inch under six feet, maybe 185 pounds when he's in shape, 200 when he's not. Light-haired, sunny, volatile, as talented as a burglar, as mad as a March hare. Now writing notes on the state of that jumping mind. After that first one in Pittsburgh, I would get another every couple of weeks or months, whenever the pressure built up, I suppose. Some on lined paper, some on blank paper, others on hotel paper. Left in my mailbox or handed to me without comment in the locker room. Unsigned or half-signed, occasionally just signed "McGrooter #45."

Once he wrote about the seasons of the year and how he reacted to them. In September, "you just want to get your bags packed for the last time and get home as fast as possible." In December, "you start getting fidgety and nervous." In February, "anxious to get back to Florida and get started again, hearing all the old jokes with the words changed around, getting back into uniform again — and seeing if it still fits."

Another time, McGraw was pitching in a game in

Chicago; the bases were loaded with one out in the bottom of the tenth inning. Later he described the moment in his print-script: "I am about as nervous as I have ever been since becoming a pro ballplayer seven years ago." He was rubbing the ball and soothing his feathers when the stadium "filled with the loudest screams you can imagine. I couldn't figure out what was going on until I peeked over to the Cubs dugout and saw that Ernie Banks was going to pinch-hit. It was his 19th season and he was coming to bat for the first time. I tried to tune off the fans, tune in how I was going to pitch to him, tune out his 19 years and 500 home runs."

Whenever one began to suspect that McGrooter might be developing into a studied or contrived personality, he had the habit of engineering some stunt or firing some mental skyrocket that reminded those around him that he probably had no equal for spur-of-the-moment behavior.

Once on Camera Day at Shea Stadium, he put on Mays's uniform shirt, blackened his face, went outside, and signed autographs — after clearing the stunt with Willie, who didn't seem charmed but said: "No problem. McGraw is McGraw."

When Henry Aaron drew close to Babe Ruth's home-run record, pitchers were polled to see how they would behave if they found themselves facing the great man with one home run short of the mark. McGraw replied that he wouldn't mind ripping one over the plate for history, then wrote a letter of explanation to the Commissioner of Baseball.

When the Mets came back from the dead in 1973 and charged from last place to first in five weeks, he bought

$348 worth of tickets for the National League play-off, stashed them in a leather briefcase that his brother Hank had made, put the briefcase under his arm when he left his house in Manhasset on Long Island, placed the bag on the roof of the car while he fished in his pocket for the keys, then drove off while the briefcase slid away onto the side of the road. Some persons go through life accident-prone; McGraw goes through life disaster-prone.

Up front, where the customers could keep an eye on him, about one game in every three ends with Number 45 on the pitcher's mound. McGraw got the telephone call from the dugout forty-two times in 1969 while the Mets were winning their first pennant, fifty-seven times the next year while they were subsiding to third place, fifty-one times the year after that (third again), and fifty-four times the year after that (third again, with feeling).

Then in 1973, the Mets started big, began to fall like flies under a frightening wave of injuries, dropped from first place in early May to last place by the end of June, stayed there two months, got horse laughs from the public and press — and then slowly, imperceptibly, began to mend. By August 22, McGraw still hadn't won anything. But on that day he did, and then in seventeen consecutive appearances he somehow had a left hand in sixteen winning games: four victories and a dozen saves.

By then, he also was the club's chief soapbox orator, flashing the old Churchill V-for-victory sign as he pirouetted in from the field shrieking, "You gotta believe!" through a locker room that could not believe its own reversal. On the last day of the season, five teams in the Eastern Division still had shots at winning the division title. On the last day plus one, McGraw relieved Seaver in the seventh inning in Wrigley Field, the Mets beat back the Cubs by 6 to 4, and the last were finally first.

A month later, after the grappling of the play-off and World Series had ended, I flew to San Diego and pieced it together with him. We talked at his Spanish-style home on top of a hill in Poway, inside the station wagon with California plates that read "TUG 45," by his neat little swimming pool, with his dog Pucci barking, his wife Phyllis fussing, and his eighteen-month-old son Mark standing on the patio table wondering what the commotion was all about.

In the living room in front of the fireplace, we kept talking while baby-sitting with Mark's three-month-old sister Cari Lynn, the kitchen phone ringing, neighborhood kids showing up to play with Mark or stare at Tug.

What we got was a fuller look at one of those modern professional athletes who are often publicized, glorified, and commercialized beyond recognition. Not only that, but a look at a runaway dual personality, an introspective extrovert, a tough relief pitcher who lives by his wits and dies by his memory, the casual clown trembling along the tightrope, superserious superflake, the wondering and pondering but magnificent screwball.

What we got, too, was a fuller look at a man who makes his living playing a child's game and the questions that seem to haunt him while he is playing that child's game — in full view of the public.

I find myself watching Tug McGraw pitch in harrowing situations — he gets paid, in fact, precisely to pitch in harrowing situations — and speculating whether the "danger" he faces in the ball yard may literally be child's play in contrast to the quandaries in his mind.

Maybe that's the key to it, and maybe he was reaching for the key when he wrote down some thoughts in May of 1970, not long after the shootings at Kent State:

"I guess it could be said that I am going through a stage in my life that is nearly impossible for me to understand . . .

"Who can I believe in? I believe in God and that is all. How do I know which is the proper way to Him? I want to know the difference between right and wrong: I don't. Sometimes you think you do because you have been brought up a certain way, the way of your parents or school, church, or country. But every morning you wake up only to discover that your parents are divorced, your school is not with it and your church is struggling, and, worst of all, your country is falling apart . . .

"It would appear that the people are screwed up.

"I really don't know in which direction to head or what to do. Why? Because I'm a people and I'm screwed up. I think the reason I love baseball so much is . . . it takes people off my mind . . ."

2

Get McGraw Ready

. . . IT TAKES PEOPLE off my mind when the telephone on
the bullpen wall rings and somebody in the dugout a
hundred yards away says: "Get McGraw ready." It
doesn't matter too much what the score is, who the other
team is, or even whose voice it is at the other end of the
hot line. McGraw gets up and gets ready.

In baseball, you hear the guys horsing around, asking
questions like: What's the difference between Gil Hodges
and Yogi Berra? And some joker can always get a laugh
by answering: six innings. In the third inning, Gil was
thinking about what he was going to do in the sixth; in
the sixth, Yogi was thinking about what he *should* have
done in the third.

That's six innings, all right, and it's also a lot of crap.
Even if you think that Gil was considered a terrific strate-
gist and Yogi is more of a tactician, a guy who does things
on the spot. All I know is that if the phone rings and the
man says to get ready, I'm McGraw, so I get ready.

I'm also nervous sometimes, like when the phone rang
in the opening game of the World Series in Oakland.

Sometimes I don't know for sure what day or month it is. But that was Saturday, the thirteenth of October 1973, seventh inning, 2 to 1, A's over the Mets. I remember all that because it was my second World Series and I was still waiting to pitch. I had a terrific seat for the first one four years earlier — in the bullpen. Now they call for the left-hander, I start warming up, and, while I'm warming up, I think: Boy, they didn't waste any time this year.

It even crossed my mind that maybe they were just getting me warmed up in case. But finally they waved me in, and I headed out of the bullpen past the stands for the infield. In Oakland, the pitchers warm up on the grass down along the outfield foul lines. The bullpen is out in the open in foul territory. And to get into the game, I had to walk past the Mets dugout behind first base and past the stands where most of the Mets family tickets were located.

That's another thing — in Oakland, you walk, you don't ride, it's so close. So I walked in past the grandstand, just a few feet past Phyllis and the other guys' wives. Usually when I'm coming into a ball game, I catch her eye and she somehow knows how I'm feeling.

This particular game, she was sitting in the second row and she could tell that I was feeling strange. Very serious, not smiling, different. After the game, she said to me, "It didn't dawn on me why you were so serious, but later I realized this was the first World Series game you ever pitched in." And I said, "Yeah, it made me nervous." Like screaming.

The thing that made it so incredible was that before the game, aside from the triple or quadruple number of writers and broadcasters trying to get to you, and aside from all the attention being paid to every move down on the field, you somehow had your mind on all the things that had ever happened to you in your life . . . all the things that led up to this. I grew up in the San Francisco Bay area, after all, and lived only twenty minutes from Oakland as a kid.

Oakland didn't have a big-league team at the time, but still you're coming back home now and you're playing in the World Series, and you could look up in the stands and among all those people you could pick out a face — you knew somebody.

As I walked — believe this or not, I'm telling the truth — I began flashing on when I was a kid in Vallejo. Then I got to the mound and said to myself: Look, this mound looks just like the one at Wilson Park.

Wilson Park is the place where we grew up playing ball in Vallejo, twenty, maybe twenty-five, miles from here, and twenty, maybe twenty-five, years back. No wonder Phyllis said I had a funny look on my face. She expected me to acknowledge her, the way I always do, but this time my face was just sort of blank. My father was sitting next to her, but I didn't acknowledge him either. Sometimes I look at my dad when he's in the stands in San Francisco and many things flash back . . . Seaver saw his father in the eighth inning of that almost-perfect game he pitched in Shea in 1969, picked him out of 50,000 people in the eighth inning when the place was going crazy. But most of the guys don't talk about that kind of thing because it sounds so corny.

Who am I? Where am I? Why am I? That's often what comes out of the blur when you're trying to narrow everything down to you and the hitter. That day, we were on national television on a Saturday afternoon, it was the World Series, and everybody was hollering and waving — and here I was all turned inside myself and dreaming about Wilson Park while Jesus Alou and Ray Fosse and Dick Green were picking out bats in the Oakland dugout.

Well, you have to be able to relax to pitch, and I feel it frees my mind of the tension when I look back that way. I can remember walking to the mound, concentrating on the hitter, and suddenly I'll drift off and start remembering things. Like the time in 1962 or '63 when I was playing American Legion ball for Post 550. Stan McWilliams was the coach and Jim Stewart was our center fielder, and I was pitching a real good game in the regional championships up in Sacramento. A guy hit a real long fly ball way back to deep, deep center field, and Jim Stewart caught the ball and rolled over and held onto the ball, and then held it up.

Later I was pitching in a game in the big leagues and a guy hit a fly ball to center field, and the center fielder made a super catch. I don't remember who it was or when it was. But I flashed on that, it was the same kind of catch Jim Stewart made.

You know, the guy hit the ball good off me, but I wasn't thinking about that so much as about the ball that other guy hit off me when I was a kid. I think the memory helped me relax, because when the next batter came up, I wasn't even worried that the previous one had blasted one off me. It's the same when I see Phyllis in the stands and the people I left tickets for. I don't believe that when a guy has to go out on a baseball field he should block *everything* out of his mind. I don't believe

it's humanly possible. It sure as hell wasn't that afternoon in Oakland.

You have to be aware of the fans, aware of the electric-
ity that comes from the stands. Before I shut out the rest
of the world, I have to be aware of what I'm doing and
who's watching me do it. Maybe it's an ego trip for me.
Maybe it is for all the other guys in the game, too. That
day in Oakland, I just took the "trip" a little sooner than
usual.

It's a strange thing, maybe a great thing. When I was a
little kid, I think I liked to be aware of the attention I got.
I had an older brother who was a super athlete, he was
everything to me growing up, but I didn't envy him, I
loved him. Maybe there was a little bit of envy. I wanted
to be as good as he was, but not because he was getting all
the attention. Just because he was my brother. He was
quite a bit larger than me. When I was a freshman in
high school, I was 4-11 and 98 pounds. When my
brother was in high school, he was 5-6 and 145 pounds.
And it stayed that way right up through the time we both
graduated.

I think I used to feel very small. I guess I even had a
complex about it. Also, I wasn't a very good student,
though I could have been if I'd applied myself (I don't
know how many times I heard that from my teacher).
But I was always looking for attention, ever since I was a
little kid. I was a showoff, I was a wisecracker, I was a
brat. Maybe it still carries over to a certain degree. But I
don't think I look for attention just for that. One day
you grow up, and you're just what you are when you get
there.

When I got there that day in Oakland — the first time

I'd been on a mound in a World Series — I had to sort out all these memories and thoughts, and then screen them out. Then it was just the hitter and me. And it was fine.

It's hard to describe yourself the way other people do . . . They see you as a nut, flake, freak, screwball. I think I'm basically an honest person. After that, very emotional. When it comes to baseball, I'm the type who overreacts — I'm positive, superhappy, delighted with situations. But if we lose, I go to the other end of the spectrum, especially if I blew it. I get real down then. Don't ask me why, it's the way I am.

Last year in May, for example, I came into a ball game in New York against Houston on a Friday night. I walked the first hitter. I think we had a good lead at the time, like 4 to 1, but I came in and walked the first guy — and the second guy — and I couldn't believe it.

I struck out Lee May, but he was the only guy I got out. Then I walked another guy, and another one after that. Four runs scored off me. I'd been pitching very well until then, with no control problems. But they took me out of the game that night, and I let it bother me, to the point where I went into a real slump — my famous slump of 1973.

I couldn't figure out what had happened to me. I couldn't even say to myself, forget about it, you're human. Tug, you're human. I wanted to figure it out, hassle it out. But I was so wild that they weren't even trying to hit my pitches. So I wanted to know what the hell had happened: *Why?*

If I'd let 4 or 5 runs score because they hit me, that

would've been a different story. But when I go in and just walk all those guys, I have to have reasons. I just couldn't chalk it off to a bad day.

But the next time out, I still hadn't found my answers. I was still looking for reasons why I had thrown the freak stuff against Houston. And when I came back two days later, they got me again. I was just aiming the ball, trying to throw strikes, worrying about walking people. I wasn't really trying to throw the ball. And that time, they hit me.

Now I began to wonder, what's the story here? I didn't have anything physically wrong with me. I shouldn't be in a slump forever. I was even calling it a "slump" too soon for my own good. So naturally I got into one for real. Started walking guys, wasn't throwing hard, and was still trying to aim the ball. Half the time when you aim the ball, you're not getting anything on it. So the hitter hits it, and the next thing you know, the coaches say you're aiming it and not throwing it. Just rare back and throw it, they say.

So now I start raring back and firing it. First I lose my "concentration," and next I lose my timing, and the whole thing snowballs. Timing goes, confidence goes. You get out there on the mound and they're ripping you whatever you do. Then you get into the clubhouse and start tearing things apart. You throw things (you don't aim them), and now the equipment manager gets sore at you, along with everybody else. You kick the balls, and the coaches get mad at you: they tell you you're going to hurt yourself. The other guys understand, but they feel you're upsetting them and everybody else. It's a goddamned mess, that's what it is.

Still, whenever the phone rang in the bullpen, I always hoped it was for me. Get McGraw ready. Give me a shot at finding what the hell was going on. But I didn't find out for a long time.

Finally there was a game up in Montreal, early in July. I came into it when we were playing catch-up ball in a close game. That is, the game was close until I got into it. They got seven runs off me in less than one inning. I gave up a grand slam to Bob Bailey. I think Tim Foli hit a double off me after that. Then John Boccabella hit a home run, I walked a couple of guys, and before somebody else got the side out, I had given up seven big ones.

Well, that was probably about as low as you could go in a "slump." I felt it couldn't get any *worse*, but I still didn't know what was wrong. I'd been playing professional ball for ten years, and I'd been playing ball since I was seven. And standing on the mound up in Montreal, I didn't have any feel for the baseball at all. I didn't have any idea how to throw the baseball. It was as though I'd never played before in my entire life. I just felt like dropping to my knees and saying: Shit, I don't know what to do. Don't know what to do. Cannot hack it anymore.

But I was also tired of being mad, tired of being upset and all chewed up. I was at anybody's mercy. Paranoia setting in, I guess. So I went to the clubhouse and just sat there and started to act like *nothing* had happened. Seven runs in less than an inning, and I could only sit there and act like nothing had happened. I didn't have the foggiest idea what in hell *to* do . . .

By the time we got home from the road trip, half the guys on the team were in traction or on the disabled list, and we were in last place, so I decided to have a little chat with Joe Badamo. He sells insurance. Insurance and motivation. I was introduced to him by Duffy Dyer, who was our only healthy catcher by then. Duffy had been introduced to him by Gil Hodges.

Joe has a way of talking about positive thinking and goals, and about believing in yourself — things like that. We'd been having meetings once or twice every home stand since 1969, when he started coming around to see Gil and Gil introduced him to some of the guys.

I told Joe what my problem was. I'd lost my feel for the ball, I told him, and they were clobbering me. We rapped a while and decided there wasn't anything wrong with me physically. But first we had to get my confidence and concentration back. The only way to do that, Joe kept saying, was to *believe* in yourself. Realize that you hadn't lost your ability. Start thinking positively. Damn the torpedoes, and all that jazz.

When he said, "You got to learn to believe in yourself," I said: "You gotta believe. That's it, I guess, you gotta believe." And he said, "Yeah, you gotta believe, start believing in yourself."

I had just been muscled for seven runs in less than an inning by the Montreal Expos, and here was Joe Badamo trying the old you-gotta-believe-in-yourself trick. I didn't know exactly what I was supposed to believe by then. But I sat there and said okay. I don't have a hell of a lot of choice. I believe.

3

You Gotta Believe

FOR A MAN at the end of his rope, I had accomplished a lot that afternoon. I had preached myself into a great frame of mind and discovered there was absolutely nothing wrong with my otherwise lousy pitching — nothing wrong, that is, in my living room. You can accomplish a lot in your living room. The only catch is that you don't get paid for it there. That ball park is still out there with a lot of guys who probably spent the same afternoon working themselves into the same great frame of mind. Or worse, with a lot of guys who didn't have to.

But when I drove over to Shea Stadium after Joe and I finished our revival meeting, I was still in that red-hot frame of mind. You know me: either high as a kite or too low to care. This was going to be the day I straightened myself out of the mess. This was going to be the day I didn't aim the ball, didn't steer the ball, didn't just fling the ball. The day *they* weren't going to sting the ball.

When the players drive up to Shea, they park their cars in right field behind the scoreboard — down the line near the bullpen. There are two gates for the players near the subway exit for the Main Street–Flushing line. A lot of fans always get to the ball park early and wait there to have a short rap with a ballplayer or to get autographs.

This day I arrived early and a bunch of fans were already waiting. They were shouting things like, "Hey, Tug, what's wrong with the Mets?" Still riding high, I hollered back: "There's nothing wrong with the Mets. You gotta believe!"

What happened was, they caught on, and they called back to me, "Yeah, you gotta believe. We believe." And one or two slightly more cynical ones said things like, "How about going out on the field now and winning one for a change?" So we had a little rap about that, and then I went in and got dressed and went out on the field. It was just a normal day — except that they started hollering again, "You gotta believe."

George Stone and Harry Parker started hollering back at them, and the next thing you know we had a group of pitchers in the outfield and I was giving a big sermon on how you gotta believe. Saying you gotta believe, not just in your mind but in your heart, and you gotta believe you want to win and believe you can win, and that kind of stuff.

It was a joke, you know. We were all laughing about it. It wasn't meant to be that serious, just something new, something different in the middle of a slump. Instead of acting sulky all the time, you can come out and act normal, be crazy, be flaky. What the hell, we were buried in the cellar at the time, everybody was down, and I was just screwing around having a good time that day. But the fans caught on to it.

After batting practice, we got into the clubhouse and it

was announced that Donald Grant, the chairman of the board of directors, wanted to have a meeting with us. He came down and wanted to give us a pep talk. When guys are in the middle of a slump and still in last place, though, pep talks don't go over too good. But Grant came down anyway and gave us a real good talk. He said, look, I know a lot of guys have been hurt, and Grote's been out, Buddy's been out, Cleon's feet have been hurting him, George Theodore's out, Staub's been hurting, and all that. But he wanted us to know the front office was aware we weren't a last-place ball club. They knew our main horses were out of action, and they considered us a big family and when somebody was hurt, it hurt them as much as it hurt us, so to speak.

And he said, I believe that when you guys get healthy, there'll still be time left for you to get healthy on the field and win this thing.

Well, damned if that didn't hit me, because I was sitting there still thinking I gotta believe, I gotta believe in myself — and he came out and snuck that "we gotta believe" in on us. He threw that at us, and I sort of caught it . . . and as soon as the meeting was over, I started running around the clubhouse to each locker hollering at guys, "Do you believe?" and "You gotta believe." And grabbing guys by the hair and pulling their heads up and yelling, "You gotta believe." And everybody thought I was crazy.

Some of the guys were laughing, and some were afraid to laugh because they thought I was mimicking Mr. Grant, and some of them were laughing *because* they thought I was mimicking him. They thought it was a riot that I'd be stupid enough to mimic the chairman of the board while he was still in the clubhouse. I really wasn't trying to mimic him at all, but he *was* still in the clubhouse. On his way out, he'd walked into the trainer's room, where he heard me, and so he asked Bob Scheffing, our general manager: "Do you think McGraw was trying to mock me?"

Scheffing said no, he didn't think I was. But I kept it up after Grant had gone. I get a little bit into these things and get to hollering and picturing myself as a southern preacher or something. I was only joking around, and if something good came out of it, that was fine.

But Ed Kranepool, who was my roommate, came over and let me know what was going on. He said, "Tug, I'd be careful. Mr. Grant might think you were making fun of him." And I said, "You think anybody would think that?" And Krane said, "Do I think it? You're damned right I think it. I'm sure of it."

So I got hold of myself and called upstairs to Mr. Grant. I got him on the house phone and said something like, "Look, some of the guys think you might have got the impression I was trying to mimic you." I was giving him the understatement of the day. But I assured him that I wasn't putting him down, and told him the story of how I had come to the ball park that day with this phrase in mind and how it was just something I was letting out. And how, during his talk, he'd mentioned that the front office believed we could win if we got healthy ballplayers back on the field in time. *They* believed. I told him how it struck me that we both thought the same thing. And I said in no way was I trying to mimic you, Mr. Grant.

You don't make a speech like this to the chairman of

the board every day. I wound up by saying that I hoped he understood. And he said he did and that he was glad I called and apologized. Okay.

Anyway, I was still in my slump and we were still in last place, but from then on we kept trying to do something about it. The ball club started experimenting with me. They had me start a game in Atlanta. Yogi figured if they could get me to pitch five or six innings and throw seventy or eighty pitches, it might just get me back in the groove. As a reliever, you always have to hurry your warm-up and pitch only an inning or two, you never get a chance to relax.

I remember, a day or two before, I had been sitting in the bullpen. The starting pitcher hadn't done too well, and neither had the first relief pitcher — but nobody ever called for McGraw that night. It was a Monday and the next day's starter, Ray Sadecki, was in the bullpen, too. They even had him up and throwing once while I sat there and wondered if I was finally in the shithouse for good.

After that game, Krane and I talked about it back in our room. We decided it was so unusual they hadn't even warmed me up that maybe something was in the works — like saving me to start a game. The next day we went to a shoe dealer in Atlanta who gives us a big break on prices, and he asked me when I was going to pitch. I told him I was a relief pitcher, not a starter. But I didn't tell him why I'd been neither a relief pitcher or starter in Atlanta that trip. Talk about an inquisitive audience.

Funny, though, when I got to the park the next day, there was a baseball — a new Spaulding — sitting in my shoe in my locker, and in baseball that means: You start.

I tried not to act too surprised, even though you're supposed to know before you come to the park that you're the pitcher. But I kidded Yogi about it and said, "Holy smoke, man, I can't start today. I just finished a bottle of John Jameson a couple of hours ago and didn't get any sleep last night either." Yogi went into his bear act. "I don't care what happened last night," he said, sort of growling it, "you're starting tonight and you better do a good job."

Actually, I had plenty of sleep the night before. But they told me they didn't want me to get into a nervous state by thinking about starting. I got kind of nervous anyway — in a hurry, because there wasn't much time to psych myself on such short notice. As I warmed up, I still felt confused. I didn't have a good feel for the ball, couldn't throw it well, felt sort of like the night in Montreal when I gave them the big seven in one inning.

I even felt strange on the mound, but then I gave myself the old pep talk: Got to fight your way out of it. Can't feel any different just because you're starting the game instead of finishing it. Get hold of yourself, beginning right now. So what happened? I got hold of myself and Ralph Garr got hold of the first pitch I threw and hit it over the center-field fence.

Delightful. Beautiful. Way to start, Number 45. At least it can't get any worse. It's an experiment: One pitch, one run. Maybe I can get the next guy out.

Later on, I gave up a couple more runs, but by then I was beginning to relax. I thought what the hell, I'll just have a ball tonight, whatever they do. Don't forget, this was back in July and we weren't making any waves. I can remember a little cat-and-mouse game I played that night with Dusty Baker, the Braves center fielder, who played with my brother Hank in the minors. Hank told me once to watch out for this guy, he's going to be a hell of a ballplayer, and he was. Clipped me for two doubles the first two times he came up that night.

But Dusty and I have good raps before games, and we're friends. So, when he came up the third time I gave him a signal that I'd have to throw one up and in — to back him away. I shook my glove at him — fastball up and in — and thought he'd understand. But he didn't get the sign and took the most vicious cut you ever saw. Here I am, trying to protect him and keep him from getting hit, and he's trying to smoke me. He popped up and didn't hurt me, but I still thought it was funny.

The guy I really cursed was Garr for hitting that home run on my first pitch. But I ended up having a fair night in spite of it, and the greatest thing of all happened after I came out of the game: We got seven runs in the ninth and won it, 8 to 7. Amazing Mets, my ass.

Afterward, the guys got more riled up than they'd been in weeks: we'd begun to think that we were never going to come out of the slump. The clubhouse man had fried chicken on the table in the locker room and we gobbled up all the beer he had, too, and went out and had a big time. We felt we had to do something crazy to get back into contention, and that night we did.

When we got to Houston just before the All-Star Game late in July, I threw for half an hour before a game, before anybody else came out to work. Just myself and Rube Walker and Joe Pignatano. I wanted to relax without anybody watching. And I threw the ball real good. They had me close my follow-through a little bit and, to stretch my arm out, I threw from 100 feet instead of sixty.

We made some improvements there, and they started me again in a game at St. Louis. I pitched five innings, gave up a couple of runs, didn't walk anybody, and had four or five strikeouts. Talk about the mixed-up millennium — they decided I threw the ball good enough *to go back to the bullpen.*

Then we headed for the West Coast. I didn't pitch in L.A., but I did relieve in San Francisco. What a blast that was. It was a Saturday afternoon and the game went extra innings — everything always seems to hit the fan when we're in San Francisco — and I pitched five or six wild ones. The bases were always loaded, guys were always in scoring position with nobody out, but somehow I kept from blowing the ball game.

In the thirteenth, though, I walked the first guy, let another guy get on base with one out, and then got the next one to hit a ground ball to shortstop. It should've been a double play. But we had Red Garrett playing short that day because Buddy Harrelson was hurt, and he wasn't used to it. He made an error, and now the Giants had men on second and third, and all of a sudden I wasn't out of the inning.

In fact, there was only one out instead of three. So Yogi elected to walk a rookie who came up to bat and let me pitch to Bobby Bonds. You could smell the second guesses all the way out on the mound. I'd handled Bonds pretty good the first couple of times around, but I was getting tired now and, besides, nobody makes a living pitching to Bobby Bonds very long. It was the first time all year that I really did wonder about one of Yogi's decisions, and so I'd have to say that I added a second guess of my own.

The idea was that we'd put the rookie on first and get Bonds to hit a grounder into a force play. But the kid we put on first had only about twenty-five at-bats in the big leagues and Bonds had more than three thousand. Sure enough, Bonds hit a grounder — but it went between third and short for a single, and they won the game.

Okay, I still had pitched real strong that day, and I think that was when I really got my confidence back. If you can pitch that strong on the road, you must be doing something right. So I got the loss, but I also got some feeling back, and part of the feeling was that maybe I was finally coming out of my well-advertised slump.

We were into August now, and it was up and down for me and the club in general. But toward the end of the month, with only a month or so left in the season, Harrelson was back at shortstop after being out with injuries for two long stretches, Felix Millan was settling down at second base, and we finally had our double-play combination back on the field. Earlier, I think, Felix had been pressing. We had gotten him from Atlanta, and he was playing with a new ball team in a new ball park: even for a guy who'd been the All-Star second-baseman it was hard.

We also had Jerry Grote back as catcher. He'd missed two months with a broken wrist. You name the disease, we had it. Grote got hurt that May day in Pittsburgh when three of our guys got hit by pitched balls in three innings, and two of the three were hurt pretty bad. What's it like to lose your first-string catcher? Ask a pro football team what it's like to lose the first-string quarterback. Before Grote got hurt in May, our staff had pitched something like five shutouts. He was out two months and in that time we had the grand total of two shutouts. Then he came back for the last two months, and we got ten.

So in the last weeks of the season, besides getting myself back into some sort of respectable shape, we got our strength back down the middle: Grote catching, Buddy at short, and Felix at second. And in center field, when Willie Mays began to show his age, Don Hahn took over and played like you couldn't believe it, catching the ball all over the place and getting clutch hits besides. Even Cleon Jones's sore feet were behaving.

I guess Jonesy must have realized that if he could put a few hundred-dollar bills in the soles of his shoes, his feet would feel a hell of a lot better. But whatever it was, we started to get the idea that we could still win a lot of money, especially since nobody else in our division was setting the world on fire. I don't think there was a guy on the club who didn't change his mind and his tune, and sometime or other start hollering, "You gotta believe, you gotta believe," like we were the long-lost doormats who'd all at once begun to breathe. I guess it was becoming the front thing for everybody to holler around.

After the All-Star Game, one writer mentioned that we'd have to play .700 ball to get back in contention, that we couldn't win a fig by playing .500 ball. But we had to get back to .500 first before we could even begin to think of winning our division. Man, we'd been living in last place for nearly two months. We had to play one game at a time, as though every game was the most important of the year. Win one and forget about it. Don't worry about the next week or month and the season or division or anything except the next game — tomorrow.

My contribution came on August 22, in a night game against the Dodgers at Shea. George Stone started for us and right away they nicked him for a run. Typical give-away stuff. Their first hitter, Dave Lopes, walked. He was forced out by Manny Mota, but Willie Davis beat out a single to third, and he can still fly. We treated Mota to third base on an error, and then he scored when Joe Ferguson flied out to center.

We got two in the fourth, though, on a walk, a couple of singles and a two-run error by Steve Garvey. Some-body else booted one for a change. But they tied it in the sixth on a double by Ferguson and a single by Garvey, who giveth and taketh in the same game. And they went ahead in the seventh on three singles and a sacrifice fly. They still had two guys on base, but Harry Parker came in for Stone, who was getting tired, and Harry headed them off at the pass.

Then, in the eighth, they got McGraw ready. I came in to get the last six outs. There was only one problem: we were still losing, 3 to 2. No kidding, we were still losing, 3 to 2, with two outs in the ninth and Cleon on second. He'd pinch-hit a single, but now there he was on second with only one out left in the game, sore feet and all.

Not only that, but the Dodgers pitcher by then was Jim Brewer, *their* screwball pitcher. But Millan kept us alive with a single past third that tied the game. Then Staub singled down the left-field line and Pete Richert came in to pitch to John Milner, who hit a rope to center for the ball game.

God, "winning pitcher: McGraw." You gotta be joking,

but I came tearing into the clubhouse after the game, screaming and hollering, "You gotta believe" like a madman. I suppose I meant you gotta believe that sooner or later you're bound to win one. Stone came up to me and said, over all the noise, "Tug, you know the first one is always the toughest." Just as though I was a rookie. And Duffy came up behind him and said, "Yeah, even if it does come at the end of August."

So officially I was out of my slump, at a time when I was beginning to think that I'd go 0-for-1973, which would've made it real tough in January when I went in and tried to get some money out of the ball club. I could picture myself saying something like, "All right, I know I didn't win any games, but I had a hell of a record for being on time to work."

The best thing was that I was back in the bullpen where I belonged, and it wasn't too much longer before the division started tightening up. We were still last on August 30, something like six and a half games out of first place. But we were creeping up, doing wild things to pull games out, and in Pittsburgh on the night of September 18 we probably did the wildest thing of all.

Seaver had started the night before, and lost. Then Jon Matlack started the second game of the series. We were playing five against the Pirates in one week, two there and three in New York, and whoever came out alive would probably have the best shot at taking the division. So now we were down three runs in the top of the ninth with only two outs to go, when the ball club suddenly came alive and scored five runs.

That was only half the fun, though. In the bottom of the ninth, the Pirates put us through the most hair-raising mess you ever saw. We had trouble in the bullpen, so Yogi elected to call in a guy named Bob Apodaca. Two weeks before, he was in the minor leagues, and after the season ended at Tidewater in Virginia he went home to Los Angeles. It took him about a week to get there, and then the Mets called him up and shagged him all the way back east. He flew all night to Pittsburgh and hadn't thrown a ball in ten days. And now he gets into this game after we score five runs in the ninth, the poor son of a bitch, shaking in his boots.

It was just one of those decisions Yogi figured he'd have to make. He wouldn't fool around with the rookie — he'd teach him right away how to get guys out. It almost worked, too, depending on which side of the field you were sitting on. Apodaca made some super pitches, but couldn't find the plate. Eight super pitches, in fact, all of them balls — and he walked the only two guys he faced.

So then Yogi brought in Buzz Capra, and he caught something from Apodaca. He couldn't find the plate either. He walked the first guy he faced and now the Pirates had the bases loaded and nobody out. But don't ever forget, Yogi was leading his usual charmed life, and there's nothing more true in baseball. Not to be believed. Capra somehow got three men out. The last one was Manny Sanguillen, who hit a soft fly to left field that took everybody's breath away.

We came home, took the next game in thirteen innings instead of nine, and broke their bats. Over the weekend, we split with St. Louis, beat Montreal, and went to Chicago with five teams still having shots at the championship. We had to win there — and we did. It could've been a five-way tie on the last weekend of the season. We were still doing screwy things like letting Matlack lose, 1 to 0, and reminding ourselves of the same old story: When we scored a lot of runs, the pitchers didn't pitch well. When they did pitch well, we stopped scoring runs.

Then it began to rain, and we were washed out of double-headers in Chicago twice that weekend. Now Pittsburgh's losing, Montreal's cooling, St. Louis is kind of hanging in there, and here we are being rained on. We can't win, we can't lose, we can't even play.

Got rained out Friday and Saturday, split two Sunday, and now it was Monday and all the other clubs in the league were finished except Pittsburgh, which had a make-up game left with San Diego — which could bollix things up if we blew two.

Anyway, we all went out that day believing we were going to win it, and believing is always easier when you've got Seaver pitching for you. But Tom was tired now because it was October and he'd been pitching since February and six full seasons for the club before that. Cleon got him a run in the second with a homer, Grote knocked in two more in the fourth with a single, Staub and Milner got a couple more in the fifth, and we peaked out with one in the seventh.

But the Cubs were nibbling away at our lead. They got two in the fifth and two more in the seventh when Rick Monday put one out. When the bullpen phone rang, it was for me.

It was hard to believe. We were ahead, 6 to 4, but we needed nine outs to end one goddamned whacky season. It was drizzly and only 1913 people had showed up — I guess the rest thought the race was never going to end.

But I was pretty hot by now, all jacked up and believing like hell, and I ended the inning by getting Don Kessinger and Billy Williams on ground balls and Ron Santo swinging.

In the eighth, Jose Cardenal nailed one, but Felix gloved it. Then Whitey Lockman sent up the bench — all the right-handers he could find. But I got both Carmen Fanzone and our old teammate, Jim Hickman, swinging, and now we were down to three outs.

Ken Rudolph led off the ninth with a single through the left side, but I fed Dave Rosello the screwjie and he didn't get it. Lockman found another right-hander in the dugout, Glenn Beckert, and he chipped a soft liner toward Milner, who cradled it like a baby and stepped on first base for a double play. He might have forgotten to step on first, but I was rushing over screaming like a banshee: I guess John decided to complete the play and end the game just to shut me up.

He didn't shut me up for long though. We piled into the little old locker room at the top of the rickety flight of stairs in Wrigley Field, and all hell broke loose in a restrained sort of way. It was slightly restrained because, even though we had just come back from the dead and won the Eastern championship, we still were supposed to play the second game of the double-header to complete the schedule.

But the umpires decided it was too wet to play the second game. So we stopped being restrained and poured it on, hollering and screaming and wondering what all the people who'd counted us out of the human race a couple of months earlier must have been thinking. They tell me that I jumped up on one of our equipment trunks with a bottle of champagne and kept screeching, "You gotta believe," with all the guys yelling back at me.

A couple of hours later, they managed to round us up and we boarded our bus for O'Hare Field. We flew back to New York in the rain, still hooting and hollering. I got hold of the microphone in the back of the plane that the stewardesses use to tell people to fasten their seat belts and I went into one of my acts, announcing screwball awards in a history-making voice.

You know, dumb things like "Workhorse of the Year Award" to Bob Apodaca, for throwing eight pitches against the Pittsburgh Pirates. "Poison Pen Award" to one or two of the writers for giving up in July. "Executive of the Year Award" to Bob Scheffing, for trading Nolan Ryan to the California Angels.

It was pretty good fun until Jerry Koosman grabbed the mike from me and did his "Hogan's Heroes" bit, the way they gave the orders of the day in the Nazi POW camps. "The starting pitchers on the Mets baseball team," he said, "give their Bullpen of the Year Award to Tug McGraw — because we would've won by twenty-five games if he hadn't screwed up all those games early in the season."

You gotta believe, I said to myself — that has to be the cheap shot of the year.

4

Left-Handers Anonymous

IF YOU LOOK IT UP in the dictionary, they start out saying things nobody could argue with, like: "Left-handed. Having more dexterity in the left hand, or using the left hand more easily than the right." And the second meaning is: "Executed with the left hand."

So far, so good. But somewhere around the fourth or fifth meanings, they slip in a few personal things, like: "Awkward, maladroit." And "Obliquely derisive, dubious, insincere." And by now, you begin to get the full picture. You also begin to understand the reason why your second-grade teacher tried to get you to quit writing lefty.

Finally, though, the dictionary gets down to brass tacks: "Turning or spiraling from right to left: counterclockwise." And now you know why no baseball scout tried to make you quit throwing a ball left-handed, no matter how you grew up to sign your contract.

I can even remember my Latin teacher saying the word originally was something like "sinister." But the thing that sticks with you most, if you happen to be a lefty, is that people also think you're sort of wild. And even in baseball, they're always expecting a "southpaw" — however *that* got into the language — to be heaving it all over the park. So, they've got you coming and going.

Are left-handers really flaky? I'll tell you, that's a right-hander's notion. If you're a left-hander, you screw up; if you're a right-hander, you make an ordinary, human, forgivable, lovable mistake. I don't know what the slant is — I almost said the "right" slant, which shows how the deck is stacked against us — but it's possible that left-handers do have a tendency to live freer. Okay, dictionary: flaky. Whatever you call it, it's still more fun being left-handed. We get more enjoyment out of life, awkward or maladroit or counterclockwise or what. And I'm not even an Aquarian.

Maybe I was always on the screwy side, but I started to get a lot more of that free living and enjoyment after I started to capitalize on being left-handed instead of apologizing for it. And nothing made me capitalize on it more than The Pitch: the screwball. Without it, I don't know where I'd be. Probably not in the Mets bullpen. Maybe still in the marines. Or pitching for the Benicia Mudhens back home in California — or the Cal Vets in Yountville.

The first time I really saw what a screwjie could do was one day in Los Angeles, when I was standing on second base, of all places. I forget how I got there — I think it was after making a base hit against the Dodgers. Then they called in Jim Brewer from their bullpen. Cleon Jones was our hitter and, while he was standing there at home plate, I watched Brewer throw him some screwballs that I just could not believe. They looked like they were going to come up and in to Cleon, but they ended up low and away, and I'd never seen anything like it. I just couldn't believe that anyone could hit them.

Ever since then, I've always noticed how other guys throw it. Freddie Norman for one. Good velocity, curve, slider, and screwball. Al Downing and Tommy John, but they don't rely on it all the time. Brewer's one of the best. And then there's Mike Marshall. He's right-handed and flaky, by anybody's definition. He throws his screwjie to left-handed hitters the way I throw mine to right-handers, and it's his best pitch. The screwjie can pay the bills.

None of us guys invented it, though. Carl Hubbell was throwing the screwball beautifully and with great control when my father was going to ball games, and Hubbell didn't invent it, either, though he sure got a lot of mile-age out of it. He was already a legend as a left-handed pitcher when I met him for the first time at an old-timers' day in Shea Stadium in 1969. We talked about the screw-ball and discovered that we threw it entirely differently. Held it differently, anyway, and we came to the conclu-sion that it's not so much how you hold it in your hand as how you release it. You know, the way a guy holds the ball, against the seams or with them, is just a matter of comfort. But what counts is the thing that gives the ball its final rotation.

I hold mine parallel to the seams . . . not exactly with the seams, but not across them, either. Where the seams are far apart, I hold my fingers parallel to them.

Do you want to know how fine we slice things some-times? If you hold the ball a certain way, it even acquires a different appearance coming up to the plate, a different "color." With the seams showing, it appears more pink or red because when you throw it, you have four main red threads that give a haze to the ball. When you throw it with the seams, instead of across them, you have two main threads that blend with the white ball and the batter sees more white. I told this to Ralph Kiner once and he said, "You've got to be joking. It always looked the same color to me." And Ralph led the National League in home runs for seven years, so maybe I'm just whistling Dixie.

I do know that the screwball is effective as hell against right-handed hitters. Your breaking ball usually bends in to them if you're a lefty, but not the screwjie. It starts in, but ends up way out there someplace. Like the dictionary says: "dubious, insincere."

The only problem with it is that you can get into the habit of throwing it too much. Then your arm and your shoulder can get tired, and you're only screwing yourself. You've got to get used to not throwing it unless you have to. Because it's such a good pitch, one of the big dangers is that you'll find yourself relying on it when you don't have to — and if you don't, your catcher will.

While I was in my slump, my famous slump, Jim Brewer watched me on television one game and noticed that I was doing some strange things. I was opening up too soon with my body and hips — when I was wheeling toward the plate — and my delivery was coming in too high. I wasn't coming "over the top" with the ball, to give it the full locker-room bit. I was losing velocity on my fastball and was getting my screwball high. And it's a pitch that has to be down to do its job.

A little while later, our player reps had a meeting during the All-Star Game break in Kansas City; Tom Seaver was there representing the Mets and Brewer was there for the Dodgers. He called Tom over and said, "Tell Tug I've been watching him on TV and he's opening up too soon. When I get in a slump, it's usually because I'm opening up too soon, and I lose speed on the fastball and the screwball gets up."

How's that for counterintelligence? Anyway, Seaver delivered the message and of course I tried to adjust. Later, when the Dodgers came into New York, Brewer asked if Tom had spoken to me, and I said yes, and we rapped about how you have to stay on top with the screwball.

Think of it this way: You're standing with your left shoulder facing a clock. When you throw a pitch, the screwball especially, you have to release it in front of you at three o'clock. You shouldn't start turning over your wrist till eleven or twelve o'clock. If you start too soon, you ball is going to be high and flat. It's basic, and it works on every other pitch, too. Think about letting the ball leave your hand at three o'clock . . . actually, you anticipate and think of letting it go at one or two o'clock, but then it goes at three.

Man, I must sound like a screwball for real. But that's what Brewer meant, and that's what I was supposed to be doing. The idea is not to overpower the batter but to keep him off balance. You can do that best if you make every pitch look the same while you're letting it fly. The minute they start sitting there looking for the screwball, you come in with an inside fastball or slider, using the same motion. Then, if he looks for that, back to the screwjie. Set him up.

And, since we're talking trade secrets, you throw the screwjie maybe a third of the time — at least I do. Mostly I'll throw fastballs. To put it in percentages, maybe 60 percent fastballs, 30 percent screwballs, and 10 percent curveballs. Nowadays I'm trying to break in the curveball more all the time so that I don't actually have to throw the screwball so much, and save the wear and tear on my arm. What the hell, it's just as effective if they look for the screwball and I throw the fastball.

When you first come into baseball, you think you've got twelve different kinds of pitches because you throw your fastball over the top, three-quarters overhand, and side-arm. That's three pitches, you think. Then you throw your curveball three ways, and now you have a drop, curveball, submarine pitch, and half-a-dozen other things. The coaches ask what you throw, and you say nine or twelve different pitches. They look at you as though you're crazy, because nobody in baseball has nine different pitches.

When I first got into pro ball in 1964, I had a fastball, a curveball, and a change-up that wasn't much good. I just threw my fastball slower, and that was my "change." I didn't have a screwball among the "nine" pitches I thought I could throw, and I didn't even have it among the three that I actually could throw. I probably didn't even think that I needed one, because the first game that I pitched was a no-hitter against the Cocoa Colt 45's in the Florida Rookie League.

Anyway, later I got sent up to Auburn in the New York–Penn League, the next highest stop on the Mets' road to fame and fortune. And up there, I came across a man named Steve Dillon, who taught me to throw a

palmball. Said it would be a good third pitch. Clyde Mc-
Cullough was the manager, and it was the end of their
season — we'd already finished our shorter one down in
Cocoa. Not bad. I'd been pitching for Vallejo Junior
College only a few months before, and now I had a great
seat on the bench while Auburn was winning the championship of the league.

That made my first summer in pro ball pretty memorable. But apart from taking the big step to the pros, the
real difference was that I was meeting guys like Steve
Dillon who could show me a few tricks.

Like the palmball. You hold the ball farther back in
your hand for that one and throw it with the same motion as the fastball. But it goes up slower. You don't
really snap it in. I needed something like the palmball
because I wasn't consistent with my curve in those days:
the hitters could lay back for my fast one and jump on it.

What I'm saying is that I needed "another pitch," as
they say. Nine wasn't enough. And *two* sure as hell
weren't. But later, after I went into the marines for a six-
month hitch, I got to spring training and found that my
arm wasn't in good throwing shape. Too many push-ups
and chin-ups down at Parris Island. I was getting my second shot at the big team by then, the Mets, much to my
complete surprise. I was still struggling to stay with them
when they got to New York. The weather was cold and
my elbow was getting stiff, to my complete horror.

It was a real shocker, because I was young and
shouldn't have had arm trouble. I was also strong, but I
knew nothing about taking care of my arm. You know,
when you're a kid back home, you just go out and chuck
the ball. Now you're one of twenty-five guys on the

payroll, you get paid twice a month, and you're chucking it at guys like Roberto Clemente.

The Mets seemed concerned but they weren't panicked the way I was. They took x rays, found nothing broken, and decided that I was suffering from tendonitis — an inflammation of the elbow. So they sent me back down to the minors for a while, this time to Jacksonville, Florida, their highest farm club. They figured that I needed to get healthy before trying to slip one past guys like Clemente and getting my head knocked off. And, after the season was over, they decided that I needed more work in the Instructional League, which is mainly for brand-new rookies and for slightly used rookies like me who are having problems.

So when the 1966 season ended, I went down there and ran into Ralph Terry, the one-time Yankee pitcher who'd been picked up by the Mets. He was working on his knuckleball, trying to get that together and also trying to get his golf game together. Terry was a fine golfer, in fact he later became a country-club pro, and we played a lot of golf together in the sun that fall. And he started to suggest that I turn the ball over when I pitched it, taking something off my fastball and turning my wrist in toward my body when I released the pitch. He showed me how it would spin, using a golf ball as a prop, and right there my screwball was born — on a golf course in Florida.

We even compared the rotation of a golf ball to the rotation of a baseball, and he put the point across. So I started experimenting with a screwball in pepper games, those little practice sessions before regular ball games where two or three guys field the ball and toss it to one guy who hits it back toward them from up close. I sneaked the screwball in during the pepper games, turning it over the way Ralph said, but I still was too shy to try it in a game.

For one thing, I got a lot of static from Sheriff Robinson, one of the Mets instructors. He said I was having enough trouble getting my fastball and curveball over the plate without trying a new pitch. You're only a kid and what the hell're you trying to do, it's not time yet for you, and all that jazz. I argued that I was replacing the palmball by turning over my fastball. I didn't even want to call the pitch a screwball yet. But they didn't want me to show it or mess with it, so I didn't try it in a game.

When I got to camp in the spring of 1967, they still didn't want me to throw the screwjie. Well, I didn't have a good spring, as things turned out, so they sent me to Jacksonville again and said I needed a full year in Triple-A. No argument from McGraw — it was a good move, because in all honesty I hadn't had enough time in the minors yet. It was down there that I started trying the screwball and I learned a lot about it. My screwjie and I were coming to terms. And it turned out to be the best year I ever had in the minors, maybe the best I've ever had. I made the All-Star team and led the league in earned-run average, just under two runs a game. Didn't win everything in sight, my record was something like ten and nine, but in the minors that's not too much of a clue to your ability. The big thing was, The Pitch started coming around.

I even started having some fun with some of the hitters like Ike Brown, who later went up to Detroit. Nobody knew I had the screwjie, I was sort of bootlegging it, and Ike would tap it or pop it down the third-base line each time I'd slip one in on him. When you throw a new pitch, they don't suspect it. Ike would think it was a fastball. He'd moan in a high-pitched voice to quit throwing that shit. McGraw, you can't throw that shit to me . . .

By the time the year was over I figured I had something. At least I didn't have a sore arm. Actually, what Ralph Terry had taught me was to rotate my arm in such a way as to get opposite rotation from every other breaking pitch. When you throw the baseball over the top of your head or ear, it makes just as much sense to turn your wrist inside-out. If you put a clock in front of you, you twist the ball toward three o'clock. It turns your whole arm all the way back to your shoulder. By the time you release it you lose some velocity, but the ball breaks away from a right-handed hitter instead of toward him the way a curve does. The fastball sometimes will tail away from the right-handed hitter, and a curve will break in to him. But this one *broke away* and destroyed his timing.

After that, it became a matter of developing the screwball and learning about myself and my arm. Terry used to throw a real good sinkerball, but they didn't call it a screwball when he threw it. But he was a right-hander, so maybe that's why they didn't call it you-know-what. The screwjie is a strange pitch, and people always associate strange things with us left-handers.

Anyway, at the beginning of 1968, the Mets coaches were still not convinced I should be throwing a screwball. All through the spring, they wouldn't let me throw it. They still wanted me to get my curveball together. So before I knew it, I wasn't throwing anything good. I was busy fighting myself and fighting them and was about to be handed a ticket back to Jacksonville again. And that's what did happen. They shipped me out before the Mets went north, and there I was back in Jacksonville all peeved and upset, because they wouldn't let me play around with my new pitch.

Maybe I brood, but I remember that Sheriff Robinson hadn't even liked the way I threw my curve back in 1966 when he saw me for the first time, and so I lost the feel of it. My brother was catching batting practice for me one day, and Sheriff tried to convince me to throw it his way. But I went back to throwing it my own way on a signal from Hank. He signed me, and I snapped off some real goods ones. And Sheriff said, "That's what I've been trying to tell you, that's the way to throw it."

My brother heard that and jumped out from behind the plate while Sheriff was still saying, *"That's* the curveball." Hank was in the habit of sticking up for his young brother anyway, and he stunned everybody by coming out and yelling, "You dumb high-school coach, that just goes to show that you don't know what you're talking about. He tried to throw it your way and couldn't, so he went back to throwing it his way and you like it. Why don't you just leave him alone and let him do his own thing."

Well, I did. But Hank wound up in the Mets' shit-house, and from then on that was his address. A few years later they traded him. After that one pop-off, he never had a real good shot. Sheriff got down on him good. One too many McGraws on his neck.

Hank did a few other things that pissed them off, too. He wore sandals and Levis, and the front office at that time wasn't ready for it. They thought ballplayers should wear Banlons and slacks. So Hank wore his Levis right into the old shithouse.

When the Mets cut me again two years later, Sheriff Robinson wasn't the only one who didn't like the way I was throwing. It was Gil Hodges' first year as manager, and he didn't like what he saw either. A young guy horsing around with a screwball. They didn't realize that I was throwing it good back in 1967. At least, that was my firm opinion — and their firm opinion was that they only wanted to see a good fastball and curveball. So when they ticketed me back to Jacksonville, I got even. I threw all curveballs trying to prove I could throw curves, and naturally I hurt my shoulder proving it.

I had met Phyllis that winter and she came down to Florida and we got married. So going back to Jacksonville wasn't a total loss. I ended up by having less of a season than I'd hoped for, but when they held the expansion draft that winter to let Montreal and San Diego in the league, Johnny Murphy protected me for the Mets after nobody had claimed me the first three rounds. In the spring of '69, I was back with them, I had a real good exhibition season, and by now they were letting me throw the screwball.

I really think they decided to let me alone and throw what I wanted and then get rid of me if it didn't work. But I did okay, and Gil even made some predictions that bucked up my confidence . . . If I could keep on improving that way and live up to my potential, I might become one of the best relief pitchers to come along in some time. Things like that. Anyway, the screwball was in.

That is, it was in as far as Hodges was concerned. But

at first the catchers didn't want to call the screwball in tough spots where I was behind the hitter in the count. They'd only go to it when I was ahead of the hitter in safe situations. I guess they didn't know if I could control the pitch. They had to build up their own confidence, too, and later they'd take a chance with it for a strikeout or a double play. It was a slow thing, nothing overnight. You're not talking about the invention of gunpowder, now; it was just my "other" pitch.

I think the thing that made me believe I could stay in the bigs with my screwjie was something that came up in Atlanta during the play-offs that October. I had Bad Henry Aaron up to bat, and I threw him three different pitches: fastball, curve, and screwball in that order. He didn't swing at any of them, which always gives you a fighting chance when Aaron's up. But I was throwing them exactly the way I wanted, and the last one was one of the best screwballs I ever threw or even imagined throwing. He just wasn't ready for it, and just stood and looked at it. I guess Henry's so good that if you catch him looking once, you start thinking you belong.

When Richie Allen was with the Dodgers, I threw him a screwball on the first pitch one day and he took a half-assed swing at it. Sometimes you get vibes from other players . . . you can communicate with facial expressions. Allen swung and looked at me as if to say, let me have another one of those things. He did it two more times and was gone, and if you're counting one strikeout at a time, I'll take it. Of course, he wasn't trying to get a base hit, he was trying to hit it out of the park and by the time I served him the screwjie for the third time, he was taking a real good rip.

I remember another time, in Philadelphia. Larry Bowa had just come up at the end of the season with the Phillies, his first trip up. He used to play with my brother in the Phillies organization, and before the game that night I ran into him around the batting cage. "What are you trying to do to me?" Larry asked. "I'm trying to get a job up here, and every time I come up, you feed me one of those screwballs of yours. Why don't you let me see some fastballs once in a while?"

I said, "Okay, Larry, you're a nice guy and you're Hank's buddy. Tell you what I'll do. Next time you come up, we'll work out a deal: If you come up in a situation where you're going to hurt me, I'll get you out any way I can. You better look for the screwjie then. But if you can't hurt me or our ball club and it won't have any effect on the game, I'll lay off the screwjie."

Anybody else might've thought I was putting him on. But Larry was so nice and trusting and hurting for a job that he said, "Hey, man, that's okay. But don't get out there and change your mind. Don't want anybody to get hurt, including me."

I said no, and then a couple of hours later there we are, coming down to the bottom of the ninth with the score like 4 to 1 in our favor. I got the first two hitters out, nobody was on base, and here comes Larry Bowa up. Duffy Dyer was our catcher that day and naturally he didn't know that we had this little gig going, so he called for the screwball. I shook him off. That wasn't too unusual. So I threw Larry the fastball, and he swung and fouled it off.

Then Duffy called for another screwball, and I shook him off again and threw Bowa a curveball that he fouled off again. When we got to one ball and two strikes, Duffy called for another screwball, but this time I had to shake him off three times, because he kept the sign on. Then he called time and came out to the mound and said, "I don't know what the hell you guys got going here, but you've got to throw a screwball." I said, "I can't throw it here, Duff." But he said, "You better. Yogi's calling the pitches from the bench."

"What's he doing calling my pitches?" I shot back. Remember now, nothing was up for grabs here, and all we needed was one strike to end the game with a three-run lead. "Here it is the last time we'll see these guys this year and we got them four to one, so what's he doing calling a screwball anyway?"

"I don't care," Duffy said, trying flawless logic on me, "he says screwball, you gotta throw it or both our asses will be in trouble."

Then he went back behind the plate and said to Bowa, "I don't know what you guys got going, but here it comes."

Bowa looked out at me as if to say, all right, I understand. So I threw the screwjie and he popped it up to the third baseman for the last out. I looked back at him, palms up, as if to say, sorry, I got to do it. And he looked back like *he* was saying, okay, I understand.

When I reached the dugout, Yogi was giving it the old way-to-go. But I was still rubbed the wrong way and embarrassed at the same time, so I kind of growled: "Goddamn it, Yog, I been throwing long enough now where I don't have to have you calling my pitches for me." And Yogi said, "Yeah, but I thought you had him set up pretty good and *had* to throw it."

So I turned out double-crossing Larry Bowa with a screwball that he didn't expect and I couldn't avoid.

The guy I *do* want to throw it to all the time, but don't, is Pete Rose. He can brainwash me from sixty feet away. It's the way he approaches the plate, the way he crouches up there and moves around all the time, the way he stares at you. He makes you think he's sitting on that damn screwball. So I end up throwing him fastballs, and he ends up hitting them to right field. Pete Rose. He sets up pitchers the way pitchers try to set up Pete Rose.

That's right. Now Rose has *me* guessing whether *he's* guessing, and the cause of it all is my screwball. My thing, my weapon, my obsession. Like somebody you have a love-hate relationship with. Can't live without it, sometimes can't live with it. Keeps me from being the star left-hander for the Benicia Mudhens. Awkward, maladroit, like the dictionary says. Turning from right to left. Double-crosses Larry Bowa, un-double-crosses Pete Rose. Great, strange pitch to have on your side in a baseball game. Ask the man who owns one.

5

Play It Again, Sister Norbert

WHEN I WAS A KID, I don't ever remember crying over a physical injury. Only over an emotional injury.

My mother was sick with a nervous condition and, before she and my father got divorced, there was a lot of screaming and hollering around the house, and it really bugged me.

If I'd finally become a psychiatrist instead of a screwball pitcher — and I can just hear you cats fooling around with *that* sentence — maybe I'd have analyzed myself as a case history. Taking my own pulse, and finding out what the hell was wrong with me.

All I know is that I promised myself that when I grew up I wouldn't have any hollering. I couldn't stand hollering or people misunderstanding each other. Making yourself clear became terrifically important to me. And maybe that's why I'm so sensitive. Or whatever I am.

Because I was a shrimp, I also always had an inferiority complex, and I became very competitive in sports because of it. I used to fight with my little brother Dennis instead of with my bigger brother Hank, and if Dennis would hit me with a rock or a hunk of board, I don't remember hitting him back. We'd be in a fight or something, but I just couldn't believe that my brother would hurt me like that. So I never cried over the physical hurt, only over the thought that he might *want* to hurt me. You put it all together and I was an emotional kid.

I remember in high school once, I was supposed to give a report in algebra. I was a sophomore and Sister Jordan was the teacher, and it was one of the few times that I'd prepared myself for an assignment. So I was all primed to give a real good report. Then I got up in front of the class and, for some goddamned reason, started giggling. Somebody else laughed and I laughed, and then I couldn't stop laughing.

Sister Jordan finally said in a cool way, why don't you sit down and we'll let somebody else give his report until you get the chuckles under control. Later, when my turn came, I got up and started laughing again, and now it really bugged me. I was embarrassed because I really wanted to give a good report, but I just couldn't quit laughing like an idiot.

I sat down at my desk again, and all of a sudden I started crying. The laughing turned to crying, just like that, and I couldn't control that either. After the class was over, I got the hell out of there, but I overheard some of the kids saying how much of a baby I was. And boy, *that* bothered me. I couldn't figure out why I was crying *or* laughing in the first place, and to do both in front of my classmates really riled me.

One time in football practice when I was a junior, I came up against a guy named Bud Kirk, who was a senior and quite a bit bigger than me. I was playing defensive

halfback and he was playing offensive end in a scrim-
mage. He caught a pass and I shot over to tackle him,
and did. But I just couldn't bring him down.

The whistle blew, but I kept trying to get him down,
holding onto his legs and straining while the coach was
blowing his whistle, trying to end the play. And the next
thing you know, Kirk got pissed off and took a swing at
me. But I still wouldn't let go of his legs, and the next
thing you know, I was crying. Just lying there with my
arms wrapped around his legs, and bawling.

It wasn't that he'd hurt me, just that I was frustrated.
The fact that he *hit* me didn't bother me at all. Just the
fact that he didn't *understand* me.

I don't know when I started to care whether people understood me, but to go back to the beginning: I was born
in Martinez, California, on August 30, 1944. If you tried
to pin that down in history, it was about eleven weeks
after the invasion of Europe in World War II. Gil
Hodges was slogging it out on an island in the Pacific
somewhere, Ted Williams was flying a marine airplane,
Henry Aaron was a ten-year-old kid in Mobile, and Casey
Stengel was a fifty-four-year-old manager with Milwaukee
in the American Association.

The only history I knew about then, though, was that
my mother's name was Mabel. Mabel McKenna was her
maiden name. My dad was working for an oil company
over in Crockett. But the first impressions I had were of
government housing and government workers: that
whole part of California around San Francisco Bay was
like one huge naval base.

Later we moved to Vallejo, which had the same tone.

Most of the people worked for the navy on Mare Island, and Vallejo was a kind of a bedroom city for San Francisco. Its population was maybe 30,000 then, with lots of young couples and kids. It was a real right-on sports town. I don't think there was ever a kid left out of a sport because there were too many people. Always room for one more in Vallejo. And that's probably the reason I made it — one reason anyway. It was a small town and I could compete.

I even competed without a baseball glove for a while because, like a lot of kids, I got a great new glove and then promptly lost it. I remember sitting down with my father when it came time for us to get our first baseball gloves, my brothers and me. I picked out a first baseman's mitt from the Sears catalogue, so we ordered it and some time later it arrived in the mail. So naturally, right away we went down to the "rec" — the recreation field, where we played baseball — and my brand new Sears glove immediately got lost or stolen.

I remember going home that day heartbroken. I went into an emotional tailspin, because I wanted the glove and couldn't understand why anybody would take it. Worse, I was supposed to try out for one of the midget teams, and now I didn't even own a glove. Well, I bailed out of that situation with the help of a friend of mine named Mouzie Gilmer, a young black dude, and long may he wave.

Mouzie came to the rescue because it seemed that his team always played before our team that summer. So when it came time for us to play, somebody didn't show up who was supposed to play, and I made the line-up and

Mouzie let me borrow his glove. It was one of those old three-fingered jobs, a right-hander's glove, of course, but what the hell.

By then, I was getting pretty good at borrowing things. We lived on Carolina Street in my grandmother's house. I started taking trumpet lessons. I remember that my dad was working as a fireman then, and I wanted him to get me a trumpet, but he couldn't afford it. So I used to borrow one from the trumpet teacher in the grammar school nearby. Unfortunately, we moved again — to slightly bigger and better things — but we moved right out from under my borrowed trumpet.

So much for my career in music. But my career in baseball probably was starting then, if a seven-year-old midget can have a "career" in anything except the circus. The coach of our baseball team in those days was Dick Bass, who worked in the Rec Department of the town in the summer and who became a damned good pro half-back for the Los Angeles Rams. I started to imitate the guys on TV, the way they swung the bat, hitched their pants, took their practice cuts, popped their bubble gum, snugged their caps onto their heads, and all that. Once I tried to imitate the TV stars by sliding home. I hit a ball between the outfielders and started racing around the bases. We didn't have fences or anything like that, and you had to run out a home run. As I rounded third base, I remembered the guys on TV sliding across the plate, so I decided to slide, too. But I didn't know *where* to slide because I'd never done it before. So I hit the dirt halfway between third and home, a long ways from no-where, and then had to crawl the rest of the way to the plate with a home run and a red face.

We didn't have a Little League, but they did have all kinds of other leagues. They had a Peanut League and, if you were a real peanut, a Junior Peanut League. By the time you got to be seventeen you moved up to American Legion ball.

But even with all those teams and leagues, I needed a little nudge to get my start. My brother Hank was eighteen months older than me and he was a good-sized kid. Dad was always bragging about him. When Hank turned twelve, he was eligible for the Peanut League, and one team wanted him to be their catcher. It was a team that was handled by two policemen, Andy Meyers and Mel Nickolai. Dad told them they could have Hank if they'd take me, too. Well, they only wanted Hank, but since they were policemen and Dad was a fireman, they cooperated. I didn't play much, but I got a uniform.

There was a black kid on the team named Carter, who lived out in Floyd Terrace, another government housing area where a lot of black people lived. Carter had a pellet gun, a pump gun. And he pumped that thing up and pulled the trigger accidentally and shot his big toe. That put him out for the rest of the season and I became the center fielder. It wasn't too great a summer for Carter, but my luck was still holding up: Dad got me on the team, Carter got me in the line-up, I was eleven years old, I had a uniform, I had a job, and that was good enough for me.

So Hank and I played together for two years until he graduated to the Big Peanuts League when he was thirteen. They never let me pitch in those days. Once, when we were getting beat real bad and they needed someone, I went in for a couple of innings. It wasn't until I got up to the Big Peanuts that they started to work me in more as a pitcher.

The best ball park in town was Wilson Park over on the south side. They had lights, and the semipro teams used to play there. Anderson Oldsmobile always had a good ball club, I remember, and Al's Sportshop. The companies put up the dough to sponsor the teams. That's the way the Green Bay Packers started. In those days, when I was still only a throw-in on my father's deal for Hank, those teams were filled with heroes for the kids in town.

We moved back to Grandma's house on Carolina Street. It was right across the street from St. Vincent's High School in Vallejo. But my brother and I went to Vallejo Junior High School. I was still too small to make the team, but I did get the job of batboy and equipment manager. My best buddy was Bob LaBelle, who was a real big guy while I was still a skinny little kid. He caught a lot of games that I later pitched; when he pitched, I played the outfield. I suppose that the most famous guy I remember from those days in school was Sylvester Stone, who had nothing to do with baseball. He did even better. Got a rock group started, now known as Sly and the Family Stone.

Vallejo wasn't a bad place at all to be a kid. But my life was turned upside-down when my parents got divorced. Shortly after, Hank switched from Vallejo High to St. Vincent's. What happened was, when they decided to split up, they thought it would be best if we went to a Catholic school to get a little extra guidance. By then, Dad had reached the point where he was working at three jobs to keep things going, and he didn't have a lot of time to spend at home.

So they switched us over across the street to St. Vincent's school. It was supposed to make up for the guidance we would lose after Mom and Dad split up. St. Vincent's was co-ed, which meant that there was a shortage of male bodies for sports, for one thing. In Hank's case, he even stayed back one grade when he switched — not because of his grades, but so he could start school as a freshman. For a year I was away from my brother as well as my parents, and it wasn't too great a time for me.

Things got worse. They changed the zoning and I had to go from Vallejo Junior High to Franklin, which put me out in the boondocks where I didn't have a big buddy or too many friends of any kind. So I spun my wheels for a year, not taking part in much of anything. But as soon as the year was over, I switched to St. Vincent's, and now, at least, I was back with my brother and across the street from our house.

Hank and I already had built our time around sports because we got a boot out of it. We were very close. But after the folks split up, we lived with Dad in our house and got even more involved in sports. What I'm saying, I guess, is that it's no joy to be little and emotional and, on top of everything, to see your parents get divorced. Just another one of those things that I was talking about — I never cried over a physical hurt, only over an emotional hurt.

Hank was my number one hero in those days. He had forty pounds and five or six inches on me, and he got into sports right away. By the time I entered St. Vincent's, he was already an established star in the high school. He had played varsity football and baseball as a freshman. I was only able to make the jayvee teams, but

I worked as the waterboy or equipment man for the varsity because it gave me a chance to hang around my brother. I used to dream about being as good as he was one day.

I think it was trying to grow up as good as Hank that gave me such a strong desire to compete. I was better than he was in a couple of things. I taught him swimming, probably because I was so light that I could float better. We used to go down to a place called Peuta Creek and dare each other to try new dives. We were very competitive between ourselves, but we still tried to help each other out. We probably had a happy life, except for the big thing, the big bust-up at home. But we were super close and happy with each other.

So much for my nerve endings. Now for my name. When I was born, I was called Frank for my father. That didn't exactly clarify things because we were already loaded with people named Frank and Hank. I have an uncle, Henry. There's my brother, Hank. A cousin, Frank. My father, Frank. And now add, Frank Edwin Jr. It caused a lot of confusion, and nobody knew who was referring to whom.

After a while they started calling me Tugger — especially when my mother used to nurse me when I was a baby and it was chow time. I guess she began calling me her little Tugger, and as time went by, everybody began using that name. While I was growing up, that's what I thought my name really was.

I remember I used to go to school, and the teacher would call the roll the first day and ask, "Now is there anybody whose name was left out?"

I'd raise my hand and say, me. And they'd say, what's

your name? Tug McGraw. They'd answer, we have a
Frank McGraw listed. So I'd say, that's my father and
he's already gone to school. No kidding, that was the
routine. I was a simple soul, but I was sure my front
name was Tug. Later on, it caught on in sports, and I
stayed Tug.

In high school, we had a football coach who was even
shorter than I was, but a lot bigger around the middle.
His name was Marv Comstock, and he was a real aggres-
sive little guy. He first came to our school when my
brother was a sophomore. He said that he'd have an un-
defeated team in three years, and he did. He demanded
respect and it was a lot of fun playing for him.

But one of the real characters who influenced me in
those days was the coach of our jayvee baseball team, Father Feehan. He was an old guy, seventy-five or seventy-
six years old maybe, who loved baseball. Used to drive a
little car around that they'd call the Brown Bomber. Our
school wasn't big enough to have a ball field, and so we'd
practice out at the fair grounds; Father Feehan would
steer the Brown Bomber out there every afternoon.

The first time I ever pitched in high school, we kind of
put on Father Feehan. Father's sight was failing a little bit
and he didn't always know what was going on; I guess he
was kind of senile. There was a kid on the jayvee team
named Bobby Hay, who was a left-handed outfielder
and a pitcher. The only thing was that he didn't want to
be a pitcher, he wanted to play the outfield. Anyway, one
day at the fair grounds, Hay and I decided to switch
the top half of our baseball uniforms. Then I took his
place and pitched the game while Hay played center
field for me. We were almost the same size, and Father

Feehan never knew we had switched. Luckily, I pitched a super ball game and we won. So we told Father later, and he thought it was a great joke. Especially since we won.

After that, I pitched and Hay played the outfield, without switching shirts. I was a sophomore then and thought I should have made the varsity, but I was flunking history and the history teacher, Rich Burt, was also the baseball coach. You take it from there. The local paper also said I missed two football games that year "while repairing some scholastic damage," so I didn't have many secrets from people even then.

It wasn't till my junior year in high school that I began pitching regularly. The best thing about making the varsity, though, was that Hank was a senior and the catcher, and he was having a great year. All kinds of scouts were following him around. Every time I'd pitch, there'd be a flock of scouts in the stands — watching Hank.

Scouts — you just know they're there, the word gets around. In those days, scouts always wore straw hats, carried clipboards, and sat near each other behind home plate. Straw hat with a feather in it, a fountain pen or pencil and pad, Banlon shirt and sports coat.

Even if you couldn't always identify a guy who was a scout, the coaches knew, and they'd tell the kids, who then told their parents. Sometimes, a scout would even call my father or the coach and ask when Hank would be in the line-up. So everybody on the team would know that they were there to watch Hank that day. In fact, the first time I remember being aware that scouts were in the stands was in high school one day when Hank was catching over in Crockett. We were playing a game against

John Swett High School, and the scouts were hot on his trail because he was a good catcher who could hit.

It made us all very nervous to be playing in front of major-league scouts. Hank was catching and I was pitching, so they had to notice me, too. And as they got more and more interested in Hank, they saw more and more of me.

Some days, it was just as well they didn't make the game. Once we were playing Vallejo High, which was the big school in town; we played them twice a year just for the heck of it. My friend Bob LaBelle was going to start that game, and when I found out I wasn't the starting pitcher, I got pissed off. The coach said he was saving me for a league game a few days later.

But I went into my tantrum act, anyway. I got mad and threw a Coke bottle in the locker room and it broke all over the place. Right after I did it, I knew that I'd made a mistake. I caught hell and was lucky they didn't pitch me out of school.

Still, it was my brother the scouts were interested in, and at the end of his senior year he signed with the Mets. Fifteen thousand for signing, the family's biggest payday. He had a lot of football offers from colleges, too, big colleges. And basketball offers from smaller ones. And baseball offers from all sizes of schools.

It was 1961, and my dad was pretty far in debt trying to pay off the loans he'd taken out to keep us in school and to help pay my mom's medical bills; he'd also lost a trucking business a while back, and that had set him back quite a few bucks. He was in debt pretty deep. So when Hank came along with good grades and a good batting average, his $15,000 bonus pulled my father out of debt.

The idea was that Hank would skip college to sign a pro contract. He helped pay my way through the rest of high school and saw that I always had good sports equipment. He just made the sacrifice.

A year later, when I was a senior, I was still small but was getting by. I really wanted a shot at signing, too, but Hank told me I wasn't ready for pro ball and, besides, the scouts weren't coming around anymore.

I asked Hank why they weren't making the rounds anymore, and he said, you're just not ready yet. Look, he told me, I didn't go to college and it might've been the wrong decision at the time. But you ought to go. It was the only decision I could've made at the time, he insisted, but I'd like to see you go to school for a few more years and get an education. So we made a deal: I'd go to junior college after I graduated and try to get an education while he tried pro ball and helped the family out. That's some kind of big brother.

As a result, I stayed in school and broadened myself, and to this day a sweet young nun named Sister Norbert probably wishes Hank had minded his own business.

Sister Norbert was the Latin teacher and the music director, and was in charge of the high school plays. For some reason, when I was a senior, she recruited me for my one big flyer into extracurricular activities that didn't involve pitching a baseball. She got me to try out for a production of *The Gondoliers,* a Gilbert and Sullivan operetta that the seniors were putting on.

I suppose she recognized me as a flake right off the bat because she cast me as Giuseppe, who was a flake in his own right. Berra wouldn't believe this now, but there I was playing Giuseppe in a musical. I had to do a gavotte and sing. I wasn't much for studying, but it was one of the main roles, and I had about a thousand lines to memorize and I didn't blow any.

In fact, I was getting pretty fascinated by everything, and even the rehearsals started to be a lot of fun. Maybe Sister Norbert thought she could harness my extra energy or tame the beast in me or something. But it's a fact that I did okay and didn't do anything to rock the boat — until the very end.

What happened was, during our first dress rehearsal we'd borrowed two crystal chandeliers from some naval officer at the base on Mare Island, and they were considered very valuable. We had to hang them from the ceiling and use them as props, which made Sister Norbert pretty nervous because they were valuable and belonged to somebody else. I guess she really started getting uptight near the end of the first act, because she would give the order to lower the chandeliers from the ceiling into place on the stage.

Well, two of the guys couldn't resist the possibilities in *that*. So, before the dress rehearsal, they went out and got a whole boxful of broken glass bottles. And when she gave the order, these two guys began to rattle the chains to lower the chandeliers and finally one of them yelled, "Look out for the chandeliers." And then they slammed the box of broken glass down on the stage.

You never saw a nun get so rattled. She'd been directing traffic down in the orchestra pit, and she climbed up over the piano and clambered onto the stage. She was frantic that we'd let the chandeliers fall and shatter all over the place. Then when she found out it was a gag, she was relieved for about two seconds, then almost had a nervous breakdown and called the whole thing off on the spot.

For a while, we thought she'd cancel the show. I guess she didn't have Father Feehan's resiliency. But we decided to go out and buy her a bunch of roses, and she finally let us go on with the show, and it came out real good. I quieted down and sang Giuseppe and didn't screw up or anything. I've always regretted a little that there were no scouts in the audience that night, either.

6

Break Out the Irish

I COULD HAVE FUN in a stalled elevator, I guess, and always could. I remember in my senior year in high school, one day I put on my fresh face and told my father: "I'm getting to be a man, and a man should be entitled to take a drink."

My father had been living with me about seventeen years then, and he knew all my tricks. So he said okay, when you come home from school this afternoon, I'll have the answer for you. When I got home, expecting a father-son talk or some kind of hassle, all I found was a fifth of John Jameson's Irish whiskey on the kitchen table.

Everything we did in those days started in a place like our kitchen or living room or out on the back porch, where I began to make some spending money by giving haircuts to the guys on our school team and other class-mates. So no matter how many flaky things I did, or how many stalled elevators I might picture myself in (with a captive audience), there was always a kitchen table — and on strategic occasions, a bottle of Irish on it.

When I graduated from St. Vincent's, I kept my deal with Hank and went into Vallejo Junior College without any interference from pro scouts. None at all. The school is called Solano Community College now, but it was Vallejo then and I started out in typical fashion by going out for the football team. I made it as an end, but I don't think the baseball coach was too impressed because I was supposed to be one of his incoming players.

But my dad reasoned things out with me, the way he did with my debut as a drinking man. Look, he told me, you want to play football, you play football. I probably didn't know it then, but there was a method to his madness, just like there was with the Irish whiskey. He was letting me find out a few things for myself under more or less ideal conditions.

Sure enough, I played football in my freshman year, offensive end and defensive back, and in the sixth game of the season against Cabrillo I hurt my back.

I was playing defensive back when it happened. Their quarterback rolled out on an option play, saw he didn't have a pass, and headed for the sidelines trying for a first down. An alley formed between the sideline and the pursuit from midfield and, while he was shooting for the yard marker, he and I met in the alley. We put our heads down and butted each other: I wound up with a concussion, a cracked vertebra, and a conviction that the baseball coach probably was right after all.

Before baseball started in the spring, though, I tried working out with the basketball team, but that was hopeless. So I did a lot of swimming and springboard diving to loosen up, and that seemed to help my back. But when the baseball season opened, my talent for trouble was still working overtime and I dislocated a finger on my pitching hand. I mean it wasn't caused by anything as simple or dumb as playing football for exercise. I did it by doing flips out of a hayloft into a pile of hay and, so help me, I missed.

What the hell was I doing in a hayloft in the first place? Well, we weren't allowed to have fraternities or sororities on campus at the time, so we belonged to a campus organization known as the Greek-letter organization. Sort of a makeshift frat, it was more of a service club, more useful and less hell-raising than a typical fraternity. The excuse for it was that we were supposed to raise money for student functions with parties and dances, and we were supposed to do things like keep the campus clean, maybe keep a bulletin board in the parking lot, help the student environment, and so on.

When our Greek-letter society decided to hold a barn dance, I was put in charge. A friend of mine had a barn out in Napa Junction north of town, with hay in it and all, just perfect for a party. So we rented it for the night and loaded it up with the local drink: something called "spody-ody," an all-inclusive mixture of wine, soda pop, liquor, beer, and assorted stuff. Some conglomeration. Spody-ody. We drank a lot of it, no real big deal, and my dad was even one of the chaperones. We planned a big barbecue with salad and all, and it was going to be quite a bash.

But we got carried away setting things up one day, swarming all over the barn and decorating it, and we started doing flips from the hayloft into a pile of hay below. McGraw naturally missed the pile of hay. One finger out of joint.

To complete the freak show, they put me in a car to drive me to the hospital in town and got held up for about ten minutes at a railroad crossing by one of those forever-long freight trains. The guy driving the car was Bob LaBelle, I think, and he jumped out and actually told the train crew that he had a guy in the car with a broken leg. So, believe it or not, they backed the train up and let us past.

Well, they drove me home first instead of to the hospital, and my dad woke up and said, "For Christ's sake, I had a dozen of those myself when I played ball. It's just a dislocated finger." But they insisted on taking me down to the hospital anyway, and a doctor in the emergency ward pulled my finger through. And when we got me back to the house, Dad was growling around, saying: "Christ sake, I coulda done that myself and saved the trip."

But the finger cost me four or five weeks of the baseball season. I did pitch the second half of the season, starting with the second game of a double-header against Cabrillo, the school we were playing when I got hurt in football. It was right out of the McGraw nut book: Mike Gaul pitched a two-hitter in the first game and I had a no-hitter going in the second until somebody dropped the other shoe.

It was in the seventh inning, and I was sitting on our bench waiting to go out to pitch the bottom half of the inning. Mike had a girl friend named Annett LaRose, whom he later married, and she leaned over from the seats and shouted: "C'mon, Tug, you got a no-hitter going, let's keep it going." So naturally the first guy I faced after that hit a double off the left-field wall, and there went my no-hitter.

I was still on the small side, maybe 5-9 and 145 pounds, and was a little wild with my pitching that year, but I had a live arm and did pretty good. Before the end of my half season the scouts were coming back, like the swallows returning to Capistrano.

After school let out, I had my first brush with the pros. It happened while I was visiting Hank down at the Mets minor league club at Salinas. I hitchhiked there and kept my record for strange behavior clean by getting a ticket for hitchhiking. Got it from some cop who tried to teach me not to hitch on the highways and threw the book at me. But after I got to Salinas, I stayed with Hank and even pitched some batting practice and shagged flies.

One day I got a phone call from Dad, who said a couple of guys named Bill Sales and Al Fontaine had been in touch with him; they were from the St. Louis Cardinals and wanted to know if I was interested in playing on a team up in Canada. I'd be with a bunch of guys from various colleges around the state and the West Coast, guys who weren't ready for pro ball yet but who were considered good prospects.

So off I went, up to the Canadian summer league for my first paycheck in baseball. It was a team coached by Ray Young, who was the freshman coach at Stanford then and later became the varsity coach. I noticed that most of the guys were from Stanford, too. We had guys like Bobby Cox (not the same Bobby Cox who played with the Yankees later), and Monty Raymond, Art Groza, and Greg Post, my roommate up there, who graduated from Stanford and became a corporation lawyer. He was a real tall guy and we nicknamed him "The Poon," short for "Harpoon."

We played for the Lethbridge team, and the Cardinals sponsored us — "paid" us might be too strong a term. We traveled to towns like Edmonton, Calgary, Saskatoon, and Moose Jaw. They gave us little side jobs to keep us from being pros officially, but we got $300 a month. We lived together in the York Hotel, which was owned by the owner of the ball club, a guy named Dan Royer. Not a real fancy place, but not bad for us.

We had twenty-three guys on the club, most of them from the Bay area, and we'd travel around on a bus, which is a lot of traveling when you're in western Canada, maybe 500 or 600 miles at a clip. It was my first time away from home and I really didn't know from anything. We'd be on a bus trip going from Lethbridge to Calgary or Edmonton and they'd stop the bus and say, you want a beer? Everybody else did, so I did. I'd order a six-pack, because that's what all the guys ordered and I figured it was the thing to do. But I didn't realize that there was a big difference in the alcohol content between Canadian beer and U.S. beer, and sometimes I wound up getting slightly smashed between bus stops.

It wasn't a bad life for a college kid. A lot of the guys used to play hearts, gin, and cribbage. Or sing along. Or sleep, if you could. I could. I used to crawl up on the luggage rack, I was so small. I'd bring a blanket from the hotel, climb up on the rack, and snooze away.

I had my nineteenth birthday up there, in August 1963. And since it was the first time I'd been away from home, my girl friend back in Vallejo was going to go over to Dad's and telephone me. That was going to be my birthday present. But even that innocent little idea turned into another fiasco in a long streak of fiascos.

We got on the phone, with me upstairs in the hotel talking to her back in California, but we began to have trouble with the hotel switchboard. They kept cutting me off and, in half an hour on the line, I got in only two or three minutes of talking. So I blew my top and started to pull the phone off the wall, finally ripping it all the way off and heaving it out the window.

I was on the third floor, and I ran downstairs, all steamed up and raging. There were these rollaway beds sitting out in the hallways, and on my way downstairs to find out what that crazy guy on the switchboard was doing to me and my birthday present, I kept shoving the beds down the stairs and all over the place.

When I finally got downstairs, I found this old guy sitting there, and I realized he just was having a problem with the switchboard and didn't know any better or mean any harm. I suddenly felt like a true shit. They almost sent me home for that caper, and I can understand why. Like I said, I was emotional as hell, and "emotional" is probably giving me the benefit of the doubt.

I still managed to pitch well enough to finish among the top pitchers in the league; then I came home and was asked to play football again. But this time I said no. The coach threw a real hook into me. He said, look, McGraw, you're not going to play pro baseball anyway. Think of all the left-handed pitchers around the country. You're not going to make it, and you're probably not going to get hurt playing football, anyway.

It was one of the few times I got cocky to an adult in a

situation like that. I told him it wasn't fair for him to try to force me to play football and, if he was that kind of guy, I didn't want to play for him, anyway. Besides, I said, I was as good as any left-handed pitcher around. How's that for an informed report? He just looked at me and laughed. A few years later, I went back and we joked about it; when I was starting the Youth Encouragement Program of Vallejo, he helped me quite a lot. He said he knew I was a good pitcher but wanted me to play football. That time, we both laughed.

Anyway, my sophomore season in baseball came around and now you might say was the moment to put up or shut up. The scouts were there and this figured to be my last year in junior college, and then what? Well, it turned out that we had a hell of a team and got all the way up to the state championships, playing against Mount San Antonio Junior College down in L.A. And I choked.

What happened was I pitched the worst game of my career, I got nailed, knocked out in the third inning. So they put me in left field, and I dropped a fly ball that cost us two runs. I was brilliant. After the game, I still expected all the scouts to come around anyway — but they didn't, not even out of curiosity. I guess they figured I just didn't have it.

I called my brother and told him what had happened. Hank wasn't overjoyed, either. But he said, why don't you give Roy Partee a ring? He was the Mets scout in our part of California and, when Hank signed, he and Mr. Partee made a gentleman's agreement. Partee would give me every consideration when the time came, he'd give me a shot. It was a little like the deal my father made ten years before with the Peanut League: take one, take both. This time, not even the Cardinals had come around to scout me, though I'd played for their team in Canada the summer before that. So Hank told me to call Partee and try to stir up some interest.

You know, you feel kind of flat and empty when you do everything to get into pro baseball, and then when you reach the jumping-off place, nobody's there to watch or say boo. Not anybody. So I put in the call to Partee, who remembered me all right, and who asked if I'd had any offers. I said no, which was probably a dumb thing to admit. But I guess all the scouts already know.

Partee asked me what had happened down in L.A., because this guy had turned in a real bad report on me. I said, criminey, I had too many good days for you to be turned off by one bad day. And I guess that sort of pried him loose, because they gave me a tryout at Salinas with Hank and the other Mets kids. Sort of a make-up exam because I said I'd just had a lousy day down in Los Angeles.

They had me throw batting practice in front of a couple of other scouts, who told me, okay, that was pretty good but that they wanted another look. Then they asked me how much I wanted for signing. I said, not as much as Hank got . . . let's say ten thousand. They said, not that much, you don't have any other offers. So I played my ace card: anything you name, I said, I just want to play pro ball. I wasn't in much of a position for the hard sell, anyway.

They gave me another tryout, up in Stockton, where the manager was Kerby Farrell, who turned out to be important to me. He just had me throw on the sidelines, then gave his approval to New York. And the word came back, give the kid $7000. No kidding, I really think Partee supplied a good recommendation because he knew I needed the money.

They already had enough left-handers in Salinas, so they sent me to the Rookie League in Florida. It didn't start till a month later because most of the guys went straight into it from school. I was supposed to get $400 a month, so when they ripped up my Salinas contract they gave me an extra $400 on my bonus while I waited out the month. I didn't have a team yet, but I was finally a pro.

When you first sign a pro contract, you have visions of the big leagues right away. "Pro ball" means the bigs to you, all the way through. You don't hear or think much about the minors. But when I signed, the California League was a pretty good place, not really shabby, and so was the Rookie League in Florida.

I got a good look at the California League during that month of waiting around, because I bought a Chevy convertible with my bonus and drove down to work out with Hank. Then I headed for Florida and my first assignment with the Mets farm teams and my first run-ins with Ken Deal, the supersleuth. Naturally, my yen for trouble went right along with me.

It was a funny setup when I finally got to Florida: all rookies and the manager, Deal. We played at Cocoa Beach, over near Cape Canaveral. The Houston Astros had built this motel-type dormitory with a cafeteria there for the rookie teams. There were two guys to a room with a bathroom between every two rooms, so four guys shared a bath. It was a pretty good setup, but most of us had never lived in a dorm except maybe in college. So myself and a guy named Gary Enserti, who got a big bonus and who lived near me in California, and Jim Lampe, who also got a big bonus, and Kevin Collins of Springfield, Massachusetts, and a rookie second baseman out of Baltimore named Fran Raley all got together and decided we weren't going to live in this dorm. We wanted an apartment in town.

Well, the manager got upset. But there was nothing in the contract that said we had to live at the complex, so we took off and set up a pad downtown. But supersleuth Deal drove down every night and took a bed check on us personally — lights out at midnight. We didn't mind the curfew so much, but we did mind the fact that he had to drive down every night to make sure we weren't cheating on it.

Once we were lying around the room at 1:00 in the morning, and the guy who'd cooked dinner had left the stove on and there was grease on the frying pan. A little late dinner after a night game, no big deal. But the smoke from the frying pan started filling up the apartment, and we all jumped up and opened the windows and doors to air things out. A little time later, Deal came by for his nightly peek and saw all the lights on and right away announced it would cost us all fifty. No explanations asked. He just didn't like it that we lived away from the complex, so he was giving us a hard nudge.

Another time, my brother Dennis arrived in the middle of the night. Just as I was helping him unpack at 2:00, Deal showed up. He made his customary speech: It'll cost you fifty. Then he drove off into the night in his big Cadillac. But I was so exasperated, so really pissed off, that I chased him down the highway in my own car. He could see me chasing him but he kept going even faster, until I finally caught up and flagged him down. He told me he didn't want to hear any excuses, all he wanted was for me to get my ass back to bed. Actually, he didn't take my money any of those times — he just liked to threaten.

I remember when I first got to Cocoa, they told us to watch out for the Florida sun, which was different from the California sun. Try not to get a burn when you come to the ball park. That was all right, but they also told us to keep away from the beach. But I went to the beach anyway one day and stayed out in the sun too long. I got back to the park that night with a terrible sunburn. All I could do was smear Noxzema all over my back, just to be able to put my uniform on and not get fined.

But it also rains a lot down there, and another day it was pouring. We called the ball park from our pad downtown. The lady said no game, it's canceled. So the five of us living outside the dormitory didn't go. A little while later, one of the guys did drive over to the ball park because he had to take care of some business there, and he buzzed us in a hurry and said, "Hey, you better get your asses out here, the game's on." We made it in time for the last out. No wonder Deal kept getting pissed off . . . Yeah, I know what you're thinking. You're thinking that McGraw blames Deal for being a heavy-handed bastard when McGraw digs his own grave about 90 percent of the time.

Most of the time, though, life was pretty good down there. None of those long-haul bus rides like up in Canada. And I was growing out of my greenhorn phase. Only a year earlier in Canada, I could remember going to Calgary once and eating out and seeing prime rib on the menu. I asked my roommate what prime rib was: it sounded pretty good. He said, come on, you got to be kidding me, but I said, no, we never ate out that much. And he said, it's a piece of roast beef with a bone. So when I got to Florida and the Mets farm system, at least I knew what prime rib was.

At the end of that summer, I called from Florida to California and had Dennis drive my car out. I told him he could bring a friend with him and I'd pay his way, too, and then fly them both back to California in time for school to start.

It turned out to be a great summer for them. Dennis drove the car cross-country for me, and he was only a junior in high school then. But as soon as he got to Florida, the family "touch" reappeared. About a week after he got there, in mid-August, I was called up to the Mets team at Auburn, New York. They wanted me right away. There wasn't time for me to drive my car from Florida to New York, so I flew; Dennis got back in the car and drove it north. As soon as he reached Auburn, the ball club left on a road trip. So I sent him and his friend to Niagara Falls. It was getting like a goddamned safari.

Then we got into the play-offs, and that prolonged my first season, too. I remember two things about those days up in Auburn in the New York–Penn League: our manager was Clyde McCullough, who was okay, and I hit my first home run in the play-offs. By then, Hank was getting excited about my finally being in pro ball, so when his season ended in California, he flew out to watch me in the play-offs.

We were going to drive home together in my car, which was getting a lot of mileage on it by now. So as soon as we were all finished at Auburn, we headed for Niagara Falls for some sightseeing, and then to Cooperstown to see the Hall of Fame: we got a boot out of that, seeing John McGraw and all the other famous players. And no, John McGraw was no relation. Then we drove to New York City, hoping to see a Mets game, especially since it was the first year of their new ball park, Shea Stadium. But the Mets were on the road. We happened to run into Jim Turner, though, the place kicker for the Jets, who came from out our way. We all drove over to the Mets offices in Manhattan and they set us up with *Yankee* tickets.

So instead of watching the Mets, we watched Mickey Mantle hit his four-hundred-fiftieth home run and saw a rookie pitcher named Mel Stottlemyre. And we saw their manager, a funny little stump of a guy named Yogi something-or-other.

The Mets decided they wanted Hank and me to play winter ball. All of a sudden, we only had time to get my car the hell back home to California, rest a couple of days, and then fly back to Florida to play in the Instructional League. I might've set a record now that I think about it: Cocoa to Auburn to St. Pete, three leagues in my first summer. But it also turned out to be the last time Hank and I ever played together, and it was kind of sad because we'd always wanted to be together. Now I gradually started to get a lot of good breaks and he started to get a lot of bad ones.

When we finally got home to Vallejo after all that horsing around the leagues, we spent a lot of time trying to figure out where we'd be playing the next spring. Hank was about three years ahead of me because I'd gone to

1956: Yogi Berra hit three home runs for the Yankees in the World
Series and Don Larsen pitched his perfect game. But back in Vallejo,
California, the Junior Peanuts All-Star team posed for posterity. Front
row, far right: Tug McGraw, twelve years old, suiting up for the
Vallejo police.

Tug McGraw

Five years later, covering home plate for St. Vincent's High School . . . "I probably had just thrown a wild pitch."

A man for all seasons returns a punt forty-eight yards.

Tug McGraw

The marines build men several
ways, some of them useless for
playing baseball, such as doing
chin-ups in field boots . . .

. . . or doing handstands and one-
arm push-ups in the clubhouse.

Tug McGraw

Dennis Burke, New York Mets

A man meets his public. Some people got the impression early in the game that he was flaky . . .

. . . to which McGrooter replies: "Who, me?"

The place is St. Petersburg, Florida, and her name is Phyllis Kline
— or was.

Opposite:
Fifty times every summer: Gil
Hodges, the big man wearing
number 14, hands Tug the ball
at the mound, with traffic on
bases and Duffy Dyer in the
mask.

There's often a great weight on
McGraw's shoulders, but this time
it's all in the family. The midget
Met is Mark McGraw.

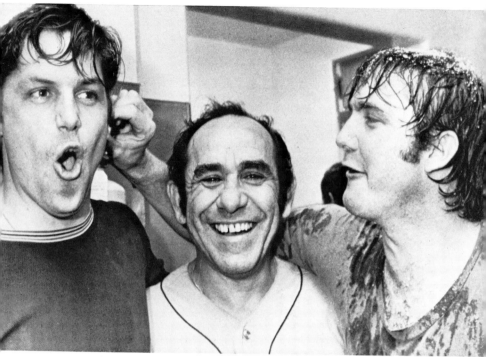

New York Mets

Tuning in Tom Seaver while Yogi Berra, after a harrowing summer, finally starts to get hysterical.

Opposite:
You gotta believe that after two months in last place you might flip your lid when you win the Eastern Division championship in Chicago on the last day of the 1973 season.

The irresistible Pete Rose and the immovable Bud Harrelson meet at second base in the play-off between the Mets and Cincinnati Reds...

. . . anything you can do, I can do better . . .

. . . and then all hell breaks loose in a melee that eventually touched off a stampede by some of the unruly customers . . .

Mets fans on their Bastille Day.

Opposite:
... and nobody can argue with a mob, not
even a hometown hero named McGraw,
when the Mets have just won the pennant.

Home is the hero: Mets sound off for McGraw in the World Series after Bert Campaneris took strike three with the bases loaded . . .

. . . while the Oakland A's roll out the red carpet for Mike Andrews, the prodigal son, back in the fold after Charles O. Finley tried to banish him to Siberia for making two errors in one inning.

On his knees, Willie Mays pleads
that Augie Donatelli, on his stomach,
called it wrong when Harrelson
crossed, on his feet.

The celebrated screwball.

junior college, at his insistence, but now we were both on the same track waiting for somebody to announce the next stop for us. And when they did one day that winter, the first announcement was for me.

We were surprised because I got the mail first, and it was different from the contract they sent me the year before. This one had red ink on top and it said "National League of Professional Baseball Clubs" and all that. We tried to figure out what the hell it was all about, and it took us about an hour to figure out that it was a big-league contract.

At first, we thought they had gotten our names mixed up. You know, it should've read Hank McGraw instead of Frank McGraw. But it had mine instead of his. And I couldn't believe it, he couldn't believe it, nobody could believe it.

It was for the minimum big-league salary: $7500, I think. Quite a raise, if it was for me, because I was making only $400 a month for the three months I'd played before that. My first year, I made $1200 and now they were saying $7500.

So we decided it was mine, and we had a big celebration. My dad broke out the Irish whiskey, and we thought about all the old days when we were growing up, when we were little kids wanting to be ballplayers. My dad got all sentimental, and kept reminding us of his old philosophy that the sun was going to come up tomorrow whether I made it or not . . . so I might as well make it.

We talked about the times when we were broke and how we'd go down to the St. Vincent DePaul Society to pick up shoes for fifty cents. And how Dad was working two jobs, as a fireman and as a janitor, and how he hurt

his back as a fireman and had to switch over and become
a plant operator with the water department. And while
we were in high school playing sports, he took the grave-
yard shift from midnight to eight in the morning so he
could always be home when we got back from school —
and so he could always watch us play. Somewhere along
the line he'd sleep.

He worked as a night watchman, special policeman,
janitor, things like that. It was hard on him, but he made
a success of it. He was a big, broad, lovable type of guy,
always liking people to have fun. About 6-3 and
240 pounds, with gray hair from the time he was thirty-
five years old. When we were in high school, he wore a
crew cut just like we did (before we went mod). And he
used to love to talk about the days when he was in high
school and how he went to college for one year: he used
to be a prizefighter and football player, and used to
roughhouse it at the beach in summertime.

We loved to hear him. My dad's brother was an alco-
holic, and it ruined *his* boxing career. So then my uncle
joined the merchant marine and went all over the world.
A very bright man, who always stayed with us when he
wasn't traveling and told us stories about Tahiti and
Japan and the South Seas. Got hooked on alcohol when
he was a boxer.

I'd see my uncle with the D.T.'s a lot of times. But I
think that was one of the good things about growing up
with Uncle Tom. He used to tell us great things and we
learned what liquor could do to you, and how not to let it.

Anyway, that's what our house was like. Hank would
bring his friends over from the high school, and I used to
give haircuts out on the enclosed back porch. We'd have

rap sessions, and growing up in our house was almost like growing up in a fraternity house. Dad was almost more like a brother than a father.

I remember we'd go up to the lake at Napa in the summertime, and Dad used to get up on the diving board — before he hurt his back — and he'd dive with us and do what we'd call the flatirons off the boards. At least, he used to call them flatirons; we used to call them cannonballs. You'd try to make a big splash, and he could do it as good as we could.

So that's what happened when we got that contract: we sat around having a few drinks of Irish whiskey and talking about those times. It was kind of unbelievable when I left to go to Florida for the Mets training camp. Only a year before we were getting ready for college baseball at Vallejo. Now here I was getting ready for the big leagues. Unbelievable.

I really can't remember much about 1965. The whole year just put me in a foggy frame of mind and kept me there — but a lot of people say I must've been that way all my life. I do remember that during the winter, I went up to Chico State College to visit my friend Bob LaBelle, who was going to school there, and I met a guy named Nelson Briles. He was taking some courses there, languages and heavy things like that, and he had just received a contract from the Cardinals and he said he was driving to spring training. The Cardinals and Mets both trained in St. Petersburg, so he invited me to go with him.

I even did some of the driving, with my usual flair. Outside Tulsa somewhere, we hit a snow and ice storm, and I lost control of the car. We spun off the road onto the shoulder, skidded through a red light with cars coming through the other side, and stopped just short of a brick wall. And Nellie said, I'm not letting any more rookie left-handers drive me to spring training anymore.

As it turned out, he later roomed with Steve Carlton, so he was stuck with another rookie left-hander besides me. Briles was a right-hander and very straight. Anyway, we finally got to St. Pete Beach and Nellie drove us up to the Colonial Inn where the Mets were staying. And Nellie just let me out of the car and all he said was, "Good luck, Lefty. See you later."

7

The Amazing Mets

IT WAS LATE FEBRUARY of 1965, Casey Stengel was three quarters of a century old, I was twenty, and the ball club had been in business three years — and had lost 340 games — when my course collided with the Mets.

It was a marriage of true minds because the Mets already had set records for slapstick comedy and fruitcake behavior. They conducted spring training on a field in Florida named for two of the greatest managers in *Yankee* history: Stengel and Miller Huggins. They hired a high-school boy from the Bronx, Ed Kranepool, to give the team some local color but apparently didn't realize just how young Krane was — until he arrived in camp with his mother. Another time, an infielder from Venezuela named Elio Chacon ignored two letters, two cables, and one raise in pay before sending the mysterious message from Caracas to Saint Petersburg: "I am waiting passage. Elio." He finally arrived a week later at 5:00 in the morning.

When they held their first training-camp game in 1962, a tall pitcher named Roger Craig arrived in midseason form after a winter of dedicated work and was named to pitch their first exhibition game. He immediately ran to the sliding pit past the outfield to work on his technique in breaking up double plays, hit the dirt, and pulled a muscle in his pitching shoulder. So they passed the honor of starting the first game to an electrical engineer named Jay Hook, who started out by pulling a muscle in *his* arm, too.

Later that first year, Craig recovered from his strained shoulder and proceeded to lose 24 games while the Mets lost 120.

So I didn't have any illusions about the type of circus I was joining, but I was loaded with illusions about the role I would play in the circus. There I was, and I didn't know whether to shit or go blind. Just didn't know what to do when Nellie Briles pulled up to the Colonial Inn, dropped me off at the Mets' hotel and turned me loose into my first — shall I say — big-league camp.

I went inside, registered and went up to my room. I still didn't know what to do now that I was there, so I came back down to the lobby. Walking through it, I saw a lot of people I didn't know, saw a lot of people I didn't even recognize, wondered what the hell I was doing there, wondered when or if anybody would tell me what to do, and finally got my ass to bed, unannounced and uninformed.

The next morning, I came downstairs and looked for the dining room, and then I did run into somebody I recognized: Al Jackson, the Mets best left-handed pitcher. I had heard of him, so at least I knew I was in the right place. He was okay. "Come on, rookie, come have breakfast with me," he said. It was a big thrill for me. I guess just having anybody say anything was a big thrill. I told him how I'd been working out every day since I got my contract, and he said, "Man, in a few years you won't be talking like that."

"Why not," I said, "didn't you work out every day?" And he said, and I didn't think he was putting me on: "Man, I haven't thrown a ball all winter."

I couldn't believe it. But I was acting so uptight and overawed that I got the impression he was putting me on anyway. I couldn't help it. I *was* uptight and overawed.

I went out to the ball park early and met Casey Stengel for the first time. My first impression was that he was shorter than I'd thought but not as old. You used to get the idea in those days that Stengel was ancient. When I met him in the locker room, he didn't have his uniform completely on, and I could see where the taxicab had hit his leg in Boston about twenty years earlier when he was managing there. I couldn't believe anybody could walk around with a leg like that, all bent and sort of gnarled. He *was* Casey Stengel, and I didn't understand why he hadn't had it — well, fixed.

There was nothing wrong with his voice though. He was talking and jabbering away, to nobody or anybody or everybody, and even to me, and it was a blast just meeting him. He had a lot of famous guys around the ball club that spring helping him run things. The Mets had forty or fifty players in camp and it did look like a circus when we all got running around on the field.

Warren Spahn was the pitching coach, Eddie Stanky was the roving coach, Yogi Berra had just been fired by the Yankees and was the first-base coach, and Jesse Owens was the *track* coach. They had a lot of famous coaches but not many famous players, and Casey would stand in the middle of all that hubbub and cover up for that little fact by hollering, "Yes, sir, come see my amazing Mets."

Well, anyway, I was amazed, even if nobody else was. I went outside and decided to act like a baseball player. They had this cage for hitting baseballs near the clubhouse, and a pitcher named Larry Bearnarth was swinging at balls that were being flipped to the plate by a machine. I stood alongside the cage watching and said nonchalantly: "Who's next?"

Larry said, "You got to get a number." And I said, innocent as a hedgehog, "Where do you get it?" He said, "In the clubhouse." So I turned around and trotted into the clubhouse, which was in a little white building with a porch. The guy in charge was the equipment manager, Nick Torman, who always went around with a sour face pretending to be pissed off at the world: you were always afraid of the guy. So I said, "Hey, Nick." And he bellowed, "What do you want?" I said, "A number for the cage. Bearnarth says I need a number."

Nick got the picture right away, so he said: "Okay, I'll find it." But about twenty minutes later, he was still poking around, doing things, going about his business, sort of acting like he was looking for a number. I finally got pissed off and charged back outside and said, "Goddamn it, I want to hit." And by now, Bearnarth was rolling around the cage, laughing and shrieking his head off.

Okay, you big bastards, have your fun. I'm here. And I'm getting paid to be here besides. In spite of all the hoopla and tricks, you get paid real good in the bigs, even the pocket money they give you in spring training. Your actual salary doesn't start until the season opens in April. At Auburn, we also got $1.50 in meal money if we traveled someplace during the season and came back the same day and $3 for overnight trips. With the Mets, $12 a day at the time, and it's gone up since then. And I managed to spend it, too.

My life changed so much that the whole year was a blur to me. I'd get up about six in the morning and run on the beach along the Gulf of Mexico, from the Colonial Inn down past the Coral Reef Hotel, maybe half a mile down and back. Then when I'd go to the park around 8:30 or so, I'd feel I had an edge on the guys. I just was all steamed up and wanted to be able to outrun everybody there. I guess I was trying to prove to myself that I belonged.

The real question, though, was whether I still belonged after the team quit Florida and headed for New York. By then, they'd cut the squad down to the twenty-five guys you could use during the big-league season, and all the rookies and a few of the older guys kind of held their breath waiting for one of the coaches to tell you the old man wanted to talk to you. The same thing happens in the football camps, and some guys get so nervous waiting for the other shoe to drop that they flip their lids. They even walk out of camp so they won't be around when the bad news is passed.

But somehow I stuck around, and I probably got some help from the rules for bonus players that the teams used to follow then. If the Mets decided to drop me down to one of their farm teams, like one of their teams in an A league, three notches below the majors — then all that another team had to do was offer me a Double-A contract and I would belong to them. In order to protect you, or protect their investment in you, they more or less had to keep you on the major-league roster.

So the Mets surprised me by protecting me, and I'd only had three months in the minors the summer before. They kept three of us rookies: Jim Bethke, Danny Napoleon, and me, and if that's what Stengel meant by "my amazing Mets," that was good enough for me. They took us north with the rest of the guys, and I didn't have the foggiest idea how they were going to use me in games. But I was just glad to be there and went along for the ride.

What I didn't know was that the Mets were going to lose 112 games that 1965 season and finish forty-seven games out of first place, so maybe I wasn't the only guy on the club who was in the wrong place at the wrong time. In those days, if you were the twenty-fifth guy on a twenty-five-man roster, you still got called into games because sometimes it took twenty-five Mets to play nine Los Angeles Dodgers. And though you were the tenth guy on a ten-man pitching staff, your number still came up goddamn fast.

Mine came up for the first time in the first game of a double-header with the San Francisco Giants at Shea: it was Easter Sunday when they called the bullpen and said, warm up McGraw. I came into the game a few minutes later with one out and the Giants had men on second and third. I don't remember who they were, but I do remember that they brought out Orlando Cepeda to pinch-hit.

I heard a lot of people shouting, and I knew it wasn't for me. I guessed the fans in New York realized that

Cepeda had been out for a long time with a knee operation, and I heard them applauding him when he came up. His bat looked like the biggest bat I'd ever seen in my life, it looked like a telephone pole, and he was a hell of a hitter, anyway. So I was unbelievably nervous, my knees shaking, all kinds of anxiety, butterflies in my stomach, as nervous as you can be.

Chris Cannizzaro was our catcher, and I remember the first pitch I threw was a curveball, for a strike. We worked the count up to two-and-two, and then I threw him a slow curve that he looked at for strike three. No shit. I jumped up in the air and started walking around like we'd just won the World Series or something. My mind was streaking all over the place, thinking that only the year before I'd been in college striking guys out — or getting smoked by guys — and here I was in the big leagues striking out Orlando Cepeda. It was super, and I was acting like a crazy man out there, and I still had to get one guy out to end the inning.

Anyway, the next guy was Hal Lanier, and he grounded one to second base and I did get out of the inning, my first inning in the bigs. They took me out a little while later in the seventh. It was a real cold day, and when I went to the dugout they gave me a cup of beef bouillon broth. But I was so nervous and shaking that I had to hold it with both hands and was still spilling it on myself.

Gus Mauch was the trainer then, always dressed like a doctor in white slacks and a white shirt, and he saw that I was in some sort of state. So he gave me a couple of tranquilizer pills to steady my nerves and said, "Take these, we might need you for the second game." I took them, but thought: "My God, do I have to go through this twice in one day?" It turned out that I didn't, but it was probably because Casey was old enough and smart enough not to take the risk.

We went to Chicago a while later and played another double-header, and this time they were going to have me pitch the second game — my first start. Naturally I didn't know what to do with myself during the first game. I mean, it was all new to me and nobody told me. But one of the writers invited me to the press room before the first game and I had a piece of blackberry pie, then watched the first game and started to psych myself into a fever for the second.

So I went to Gus and said, "Look, I'm real nervous. Why don't you give me one of those tranquilizer jobs to calm me down so I can pitch?" Gus probably thought he'd have to tranquilize me every time Stengel pitched me. But he gave me one of them and I think it calmed me down too much. All I could see in front of me was that fucking blackberry pie. Billy Williams hit a three-run home run off me and I never made it through the first inning.

I didn't take any more tranquilizers that season, but it wasn't because I suddenly became serene. No way. I still felt lucky any time I did something right. One thing I did right was finally win a game. Pitched six or seven innings against St. Louis on August 22 and we beat them, 4 to 2. Then four days later, I started a game against Sandy Koufax. The Mets had never beaten him. In fact, in those days they'd play eighteen games against the Dodgers every summer and lose sixteen of them. But this night, the Mets and McGraw ripped one off.

I remember we were ahead, 3 to 2, in the seventh when Wes Parker hit a triple off the fence in right-center. There was the tying run on third with two outs and everybody thinking the Mets were ready for their nightly swoon. But Jack Fisher, who was our number one starting pitcher, was called in from the bullpen to relieve me, that's how bad the Mets wanted to win it. John Roseboro was the hitter, but Fisher got him out, and then in the eighth, Ron Swoboda and Joe Christopher hit back-to-back home runs for us, and we beat them, 5 to 2.

Koufax was taken out of the ball game right after I was, but we were what they call "the pitchers of record," so I stayed out on the bench and watched Fisher get out of the inning. Then they sent me to the clubhouse to get rid of my wet stuff — my game clothes — and I was still there when the game ended. It was unreal, beating Koufax, because it was my second straight win and he was Koufax, he was the best, he'd won the Cy Young Award and twenty-five games and everything. So I started jumping up and down when it ended, going crazy as usual, but this time the rest of the guys didn't shake their heads or anything, and nobody went around the locker room saying McGraw's some strange cat.

We went down to Williamsport, Pennsylvania, that summer to play an exhibition game against the Mets farm team; that's where my brother Hank had been sent from the minor leagues' spring training camp. We hadn't seen each other since the spring, and it was really a super scene. He was having a good year down there, but I was in the bigs, and that was what was important. When I got out to where Hank was staying, we ran up to each other and hugged and cried. If you ask me if other brothers carry on like that, I don't know. We do, and we always did, and it's because we come from a family with nerve endings out to there.

It was also funny, because they'd written in the local paper that the McGraw brothers were going to play against each other that night: would Hank be able to get a hit off his little brother? Well, it wasn't the end of the world, even in Williamsport. But since they were getting all worked up over it, I thought I'd add a little spice to the menu. I made a statement that I was going to knock him on his ass at the plate. The papers were making a big deal of it, and we had it all set up.

What happened was, he came up to bat the first time and the first pitch I threw really knocked him on his ass. He knew I was going to brush him back, but not knock him on his ass. I mean, I'd mentioned to him that I'd have to move him away. But I overplayed my hand or something, and the ball took off and damned near zapped him. I was scared at first, but he was okay and then he got up, dusted off his pants without complaining, and popped up.

The next time up, though, he hit a double off the left-field wall. And after the game, everybody thought I'd told him what was coming just to make him look good so that maybe the Mets would be impressed and bring him up. But it wasn't true at all, not that time; he just smoked me.

I'm big for "firsts," and everything that happened that year was one because it was my first swing around the big leagues. Even now, I can be pitching in a game, maybe surrounded by all kinds of trouble, and I'll think back to something that happened the first time: like, the first time I pitched surrounded by all kinds of trouble. First day in spring training. First appearance as a relief pitcher with the Mets. First start. First win, first loss.

First road trip, and what I remember about that was I forgot to bring my baseball hat. I was scheduled to pitch, too. Warren Spahn got pissed off and said I'd have to borrow somebody else's hat to pitch, and the next time I forgot it, he'd fine me. So the next trip I remembered my hat but forgot my shoes.

Spahn was so different from me, it was unbelievable. He was terrifically organized, I was scattered around. He was strict, I was loose as a goose. He was calm and poised, I was coming apart at my mental seams half the time. He was right, I was wrong. He even said, "Look, I'm not going to narrow it down to items of clothing. The next time you forget *anything,* you're fined." And that kind of cured me. I didn't forget too many things after that. It was just that I was usually so frantic to get on the team bus, I was so nervous about it, that I didn't always think of the necessities I was supposed to bring with me.

My roommate then was Swoboda, and he was quite a character, too. How they ever put two guys like us together, I'll never know, but they did and we had one of the brighter rooms on the road list of our traveling secretary, Lou Niss. Maybe "brighter" isn't the right word. Swoboda and I were around the clubhouse one day that season and we got to squirting soda-pop bottles — we got a squirt war going for some reason, don't ask me what it was. When you were a kid you'd shake up a soda-pop bottle and put your thumb on top and squirt it. I had some kind of strawberry pop and he had Coke or something, and we started squirting.

You put your thumb on the top and it's supposed to zip out the right side, like a goddamn laser beam. But somehow it came out the wrong side this time, and it squirted all over Swoboda and into Spahn's locker behind him. All over a clean white shirt Spahn had just taken off and hung up when he put on his uniform. And don't forget, Spahnie was my coach, my hero, my opposite, my boss, and a sharp and careful dresser besides.

He came in just then, looked at the shirt, saw me standing there with the pop bottle in my hand, and started cursing and hollering. How the hell, he asked, did I get to the big leagues with that hatrack I had for a head. I don't know when they started calling Swoboda "Rocky," but it might've been after he and I teamed up on a couple of capers like that one. By then, though, I had long since been ranked as one of the coming superflakes of the clubhouse, and you couldn't have changed me with a Sherman tank.

I had real hang-ups partly because I didn't feel like I belonged at that level yet. I knew I was there because of the rules: The Mets could either keep me or risk losing me to some other team. I was the shortie again, like when I was a kid back home and my father or brother would con some coach into letting me hang around the team. Now I couldn't fake my way, not in the bigs. I'd do real well for five or six innings maybe, then the third time around the batting order I'd say to myself, "These guys have seen everything I throw. Now they're going to get me. Man, he's on me now." And I'd begin to over-throw, get knocked out of the box, and wouldn't be there the fourth time around. I'd been brought up too soon and too quick.

I remember another "first" that summer: first time I got kicked out of a game. It happened in September in my last start before leaving for boot camp in the marines. It was in Pittsburgh, and my brother was in the stands, so I wanted to be really sharp. Before the game, some of the guys got to talking and somebody mentioned that a no-hitter had never been pitched there in Forbes Field. Right away my mind began to twirl. I went out and just thought, maybe I'll be the first.

For three innings, it looked like I might be on my way: no hits, no runs, not even any walks. In the fourth, I got the first guy out, making ten in a row, but then somebody booted one for an error and the string was broken. Okay, in those days, a booted grounder was no novelty on the Mets. But I began to build up some juice after I walked the next guy and Clemente hit a ball that skipped right the hell off home plate. It bounced way up in the air and I had to wait for it to come down. By the time I fielded it, I had no play at first and he beat it out.

Now on three straight plays, I lost my little perfect game and my no-hitter, and they had the bases loaded with one down besides. They still hadn't scored, but all my fantasies were out the window and I was getting pissed off, too. The next thing that happened was that Donn Clendenon came up. He told me later (after he was traded to the Mets) that he always knew when I was going to throw my curve. So now I threw him what I thought was a real good curve, ankle low, but he jumped on it and ripped it through my legs, so hard I was lucky he didn't castrate me.

It went through into center field and took two mean hops toward Jim Hickman, who came charging in trying to throw the first-base runner out at second. But these were the days when the Mets were the clowns of baseball, and he overran the ball. I mean he was coming in and the ball was going out, and it shot past him. They kept the batting cage in center field then, it was like 460 feet from the plate, and the ball rolled all the way out there to the cage.

Hickman turned around and charged back after it — the Mets didn't believe in backing up anybody in those days. But now the runners were tearing around the bases like crazy, so the throw from Hickman was relayed to third base, where I was standing a few yards behind the bag backing it up. Sure enough, the cutoff man, the guy handling the relay, threw the ball in the direction of third but he overthrew it, as though he was aiming for me all the time.

So I caught the ball on the fly and, with nobody to tag out there on the grass in foul territory, I turned and fired it home. Okay, I made a wild throw toward the catcher, Greg Goossen, who'd just been called up from the minors, but he couldn't see where the hell the ball was anyway because the runner was in his path. It got past Goossen and he turned around and went running over by the dugout trying to flag it down, so I charged from third in to the plate . . . I was not only the guy who started the whole mess by pitching the ball but also the guy who was ending it by covering two bases.

Now I was covering home against the only runner for the Pirates who hadn't scored, Clendenon, the guy who hit the ball in the first place. And when Goossen finally got it and ripped it back to me at the plate, I whirled around to tag him — too late. Three errors and four runs on one screwed-up play.

I started cursing and jumping up and down, I was completely frustrated and wild, cursing the world, not anybody in particular. But it happened that the umpire was standing beside me, so he thumbed me out of the game. I couldn't understand why, and he couldn't understand me. The coaches came out to calm me down, but finally I decided to leave, and did. But in order to get to the visiting clubhouse in Forbes Field, you had to go through the home dugout. And those guys thought it was a riot, this kid left-hander blowing his top, and so when I went through the dugout they all started to razz me and rip me.

Clendenon needled me good, and asked me, as though he really had an interest in getting the facts straight: "Who were you cussin'?" I said, "I cussed him up and down. But I didn't mean him," and I tipped my head toward the umpire. "Who did you mean?" Clendenon said, having a ball. And I just stomped past him and answered, "You, you son of a bitch."

Then I got sort of scared and ran into the clubhouse.

One other thing happened that summer, and it was a "first" for me, too: Casey fell down and broke his left hip and had to be replaced as manager by Wes Westrum, and that was the first time any of us had known a seventy-five-year-old manager to fall down and break his hip.

I was sorry because I liked the old man, even though I

had had hardly any conversations with him. He just sort of conversed with the world. But he was always on the ball. Once, the sister of a buddy from high school and four of her girl friends decided to come to New York. They visited the ball park, and I showed them around. Casey was out there early and he took over the party, talking to the girls in that courtly style of his, like the 1890s or something, and getting a lot of laughs, like he was a ladies' man and McGraw's friends were worth his best shot.

Another time, Krane and I were chucking baseballs to Dick Stuart, the first baseman who could hit the ball but couldn't catch it. They called him Dr. Strangeglove, he was so bad. But this time, Case was sounding off about how amazing we all were and he said out loud: "Mister McGraw there, he's got the earmarks of a splendid big-league pitcher. When he's got two-and-two on the batter, you might get a foul off him."

So it was kind of sad when Casey finally limped away on a crooked cane that summer and Westrum took over. It was a big change. Stengel was always in the middle of everything, but Wes was a real loner. He used to talk to the players as though we were the only audience, the way Casey used to talk to the public. Wes also had some "motivation" ideas of his own, but they weren't exactly the same sort I started to come up with later. Not so much "you gotta believe," but more like "you gotta perceive."

He put a notice up on the bulletin board in the clubhouse with the title, "How Many Points Do You Have?" And he told us to look in the mirror every day and ask ourselves how many of these points we felt we honestly had:

1. "The desire to win dominates."
2. Ability to run.
3. Ability to throw.
4. Ability to hit.
5. Aggressiveness and hustle.
6. Leadership.
7. Intelligence.
8. Ability to field.
9. Team play.
10. Emotional stability.
11. Good condition.
12. Good sportsmanship.
13. Knowledge of rules.

I knew I could throw and run, and even hit. I'm not too sure I would've qualified under "emotional stability." But nobody snickered or anything, because the guys realized he was trying to say a few things, even if it was a hell of a switch from Casey Stengel. Westrum carried a poem around in his wallet, something that a fan had sent him years before when he was a catcher with the Giants, and part of it said:

> Think big and your deeds will grow
> Think small and you'll fall behind;
> Think that you can, and you will;
> It's all in a state of mind.
>
> If you think you are outclassed, you are;
> You've got to think high to rise;
> You've got to be sure of yourself before
> You can ever win a prize.
>
> Life's battles don't always go
> To the stronger or faster man,
> But sooner or later, the man who wins
> Is the fellow who thinks that he can.

Don't knock it. The only problem, though, was that if you were a Met in those days, you didn't usually look in the mirror after getting clobbered and ask yourself thirteen questions. Or how big were you thinking that afternoon. You usually asked yourself what the hell had gone wrong, and then you shaved your face.

8

Hawks, Doves, and Brothers

MY KID BROTHER DENNIS was a dedicated twenty-year-old
"dove" and the leader of the antiwar group on the
campus back home in Vallejo when I went into the
marines and became a trained counterguerrilla fighter.

It was in September 1965, the day after I got thrown
out of the game in Pittsburgh. The war in Vietnam was
heating up and hadn't even reached its peak yet, but it
was already putting a lot of distance between people like
Dennis and me.

I was kind of a dove myself, at least as far as the way we
were going about the war. I mean, I believed in our
"cause," and I was against communism, and I was sure
that the war would go on someplace else even if the
United States won a military victory. But in eighteen
months, I had gone from the campus back home into pro
baseball, I had met Casey Stengel, made the Mets, and
beaten Sandy Koufax — and all of a sudden now I was
heading for some hellhole called Parris Island, where I
would be dressed in green fatigues, drilled out of my
mind, and drummed into the life of a "pickle." So I guess

you would have to say I was neither a hawk nor a dove. I was just undecided.

To keep it all in the family, my older brother Hank drove me to the airport early in the morning when I left the Mets to join the marines. Me and Jim Bethke, another rookie pitcher, both of us going in for a six-month hitch that hopefully would end sometime during the next spring training. We were investing our winter in the marines in order not to miss any of the next season. But neither Bethke nor I knew that day that we would be two different, shook-up guys by the time we threw another baseball. Older and wiser and sadder, that would cover it.

Sometimes during a ball game now I'll remember some grinding thing that happened to me in the marines. And I realize that those six months in service left me with a lot of scars and bruises. Emotional ones, like when my folks split up or when I couldn't get people to understand something I was trying to do. They also left me tougher in some ways. But I'm no psychologist, so I'm not going to try to "sum it all up."

Bethke and I were both pretty scared that morning. We'd heard all sorts of stories, wild stories, about the life in boot camp under the drill instructors. We'd heard how six recruits had drowned down there on Parris Island one night during a march, and it was horrifying to realize that we were headed for the same place with the same discipline and the same ball-breaking D.I.s.

Actually, Bethke and I started to brace ourselves for the marines by getting into shape before we got there. Chances are, we were already in a hell of a lot better shape than the average guy who goes into the marines

cold. But we got the feeling that physical discipline was
the nut of the problem, so we worked extra hard during
our last few weeks before we parted company with Wes
Westrum and the slaphappy Mets.

Well, Parris Island turned out to be scary, all right.
The D.I.s started hollering and screaming at us the minute we arrived, and I suppose they did it just to shake us
up. A guy named Sergeant G. M. Early was my drill instructor. He was a staff sergeant at the time, and he
turned out to be a super guy. He didn't go overboard
with the hard-core, old-corps discipline or tactics, but he
also didn't leave anything to our imagination either.

We had a platoon of guys mostly from New York, and
three or four ballplayers were in our "platoon series," as
they called it. We were really the long and the tall and
the short, the fat and the small. We stayed up till 3:00
every morning for a while, just making our bunks the
right way and learning spectacular things like drawing
the sheets across the bunks as tight as hell and getting the
blankets perfect. Every time somebody did his bunk and
it wasn't exactly the way the D.I. wanted it, he'd make us
all tear up our bunks — to show who was boss.

By the time we quit screwing around with that and got
into those perfectly made bunks to sleep, it was 2:30 or
3:00. Then they'd haul us out at 4:30 to start the next
day. A week before that, I'd been lounging in the lobbies
of the best hotels in the National League or tossing my
laundry into a bucket in the locker room of a big-league
baseball team. Now they were systematically hammering
me into a zombie, and I couldn't believe it.

At times they wouldn't even let us use the head for
three or four days in a row. That was the drill, you were

supposed to indoctrinate your kidneys. They'd issued us new gear, shower soap, toothbrush, toothpaste, all the stuff in plastic bags, and one of my first memories of Parris Island, South Carolina, is what happened to a guy who tried to bootleg one of those plastic bags when the ordeal got too heavy for him.

He was a real strong black dude from the Virgin Islands. But man, after three or four days of not letting us go to the bathroom, it was getting incredible. And on top of it all, the drill instructors were pulling a barracks inspection while we were all squirming around trying to stand at attention, as though nothing was different.

We were standing in front of our bunks, actually, when this guy just couldn't hold it any longer. He took out one of those plastic bags while the sergeant was entering the barracks at the other end, and he popped the bag and started pissing in it. We all wanted to crack up, because it was so goddamned hilarious in a sick sort of way. But we were still too scared, because we knew that if he got caught, they'd kill him, or make him wish he had been killed.

But this guy was too far gone to worry about things like military discipline or the Code of Military Justice. He just had to take a three-day piss, and that was that. Then when he did, he just went from one problem to another. Now he had a plastic bag all filled, and didn't know what the hell to do with it. He tried to stuff it in his pocket before the D.I. noticed him, but by now the front of his uniform was all wet and the D.I. asked without any preliminaries, "What's going on here?" The guy said, "Nothing, sir," which wasn't exactly the truth by a long shot. So the D.I. popped his hand against the guy's pocket and the bag busted all over both of them.

Man, there was hell to pay over that, and I wouldn't be too surprised if they *still* have that poor son of a bitch walking tours with a rifle or double-timing his ass all over South Carolina. I mean, that's an *infraction.*

Another time, we got issued rifles before going to the firing range and brought them back to what they called "squad bay," standing at attention in front of our bunks. The D.I. was talking to someone at the other end of the bay and this guy named Goldstein just couldn't resist the temptation to draw a bead on him. He didn't have any ammo — he just wanted the thrill of pointing the empty gun at the D.I. because he was the monkey on our backs twenty-four hours a day.

Just then, the assistant D.I. walked in the back door, but Goldstein was too busy getting the sergeant in his sights and didn't notice who was watching him. The assistant D.I. kicked the rifle out of his hand with one flying boot and started bawling, "Sergeant Early! Sergeant Early! Do you see what this guy's doing? He's trying to kill you, for God's sake." And then they both came after that poor guy, hollering and screaming at him, and they just did a number on Goldstein that you couldn't believe.

The assistant was named Sergeant Henderson, a little guy but strong and gung-ho. He'd wanted to be in the marines from five years old, and he loved the corps — loved it at the top of his lungs. When they got finished with Goldstein, that poor slob wrote home and said, come get me out. He and another guy in the platoon used to screw everything up. They just weren't cut out for the service, couldn't get their rifles back together or polish brass or shoes. They got so rattled whenever anybody hollered at them that they used to fall apart. In marching drill, they'd take the wrong turn and go the wrong way, just like in a comedy. They were super guys, but they just weren't cut out for the military life. Luckily, they were in the reserves like we were and weren't in for a three-year hitch. They gave us some laughs, but they wouldn't have lasted too long in a war.

I guess the most important thing that happened to me personally was at the rifle range. To the marines in camp, that was the main event. We had guys go crazy if they didn't qualify with a rifle, everybody made such a religion out of it. Any other job comes second, they kept telling us, and if you don't qualify at that, it's the worst thing in the universe. They'd make you feel you weren't a human being. Guys had tried to kill themselves when they didn't qualify, like they'd deserted in the face of the enemy or something scandalous like that.

I was really sweating it out, too, because they wouldn't let me shoot left-handed, and I'd never shot right-handed before. But I sweated and strained and squinted and got lucky, and I barely did qualify. That was the biggest hurdle in a world that seemed crammed with hurdles.

When I first got to boot camp, they'd give everybody a test to see if you'd qualify for officers school, pilot school, helicopter school, or whatever. The C.O. called me in and asked me about officers school. I said I'd just as soon get out of the corps when my six months ended and get back to baseball. He tried hard to convince me that a baseball career wasn't secure enough, you could get injured and all that. I couldn't believe what he was arguing: In my mind, all those lieutenants were leading guys up the hill and getting killed, and here he was putting the knock on baseball. I'd qualified for OCS, but I couldn't see myself as a new lieutenant in the security of a hill in Vietnam.

The D.I.s knew some of us were baseball players, too, but instead of trying to talk us out of it, they tried to cash in on it.

Every Sunday we had field-day meets, with platoons and companies and battalions all in one big Sunday Olympics. They'd have a track meet that combined regular track events with marine events like push-ups, chins, obstacles, rope-climbing, fireman's carry, and distance running. After a while, it got to be a personal war between me and a guy from the Pittsburgh Pirates minor-league organization, Wayne White. In civilian life, believe me, he'd qualify as an official flake in McGraw's class.

Every Sunday, he'd show up in a different platoon, and the D.I.s would put us up against each other in all the events for a case of beer. We were the star performers, or the guinea pigs, and we happened to be evenly matched. But our own D.I. would want to beat the shit out of us if we lost, because it meant they also lost a case of beer. They were true humanitarians.

Bethke and I were still near each other at Parris Island and we even ran on the same two-mile relay team; he ran next-to-last and I ran the anchor leg. He had a lot of stamina, but I could sprint the hundred and was probably in better shape than most of the guys.

The last Sunday before we graduated from boot camp, they held the big battalion meet, and I tried out for the quarter-mile relay and the hundred-yard dash and made them both. There were maybe 800 or 900 guys in a training battalion, and they were all out there howling while dozens of us competed in these events. I started out pretty hot, finishing third in the hundred-yard dash, which wasn't bad considering that I was never known as fast in high school. But with the D.I. betting his case of beer on you, you have resources that you didn't even know you had.

In the relay race, though, I screwed up in a memorable way. You know, beneath that marine green, McGrooter was the same old lovable weirdo. I ran the anchor leg, the last of the four on our team, but somehow in my frenzy to grab the baton from the other guy and get going, I dropped it. Well, maybe the other guy dropped it while he was trying to pass it to me. Anyway, *one* of us dropped it, and our team lost a lot of time and ground. So I did the only thing that I could: I ran my ass off.

The D.I. had given us a special drink of syrup and water and other stuff that was supposed to supply us with energy. But even with the special energy drink, we finished way the hell back because the other guy and I fumbled the baton. Not only that, but by the time I was going into the far turn, I was all pooped out from sprinting to make up the lost ground. But all the guys got up out of the bleachers and ran down to the track to yell, and the D.I. was hollering things like "McGraw, you better move your ass, you son of a bitch." And there I was coming down the back stretch, and by then he was practically chasing me into the home stretch, hollering at me. I must've made up a hundred yards on the other guys,

but we still finished last, and then I had to drag myself
back to where everybody was while the sergeant was
screaming at me from about three inches off my right
ear.

I was sort of amused. The Met tradition, I thought to
myself, lives in South Carolina.

If there was any real change for me in the marines, it
was probably in my relations with people. You are just
there on your own, that's number one. For the first time
in my life, no teammates. No brothers. No family. No
nothing. It was a hell of an experience, especially for
somebody as emotional and dependent as me. What I
think happened was that I got to know myself better, got
more control over myself. Anyway, whether I could control it or not, I was beginning to find out what made me
tick.

Maybe you have to be low to understand "high," or be
poor before you can appreciate "rich." Maybe I had to
spend some time in this particular trap in order to latch
onto the opportunity of my "free" life back home. In a
mud hole somewhere the hell out there in bivouac country, the uncertainties of civilian life seem like lollipops.
And compared with the average drill instructor, Ken
Deal and Sheriff Robinson seemed like a pair of easy
aces.

In boot camp, they had us so psyched out and brain-
washed that we would've done anything on command —
which was the idea, I suppose. They send you to in-
fantry training after you go through that zombie phase,
they send you into the grunts, into the field marines to
learn things called "general warfare," "jungle tactics" and

"guerrilla warfare." I've forgotten it all by now, but in those days they made you feel that you could subsist by killing if you had to.

It was strange and frightening to think that you could learn all those things and that you might have to use them, reaching back for them the way you reach back for your fastball in a game. But the marines drag you down and strip you of everything you ever learned in the past. You forget to think for yourself: The only judgment you have finally is an *order*. You're a *pickle* in a green uniform, and somebody else does the thinking for you and communicates it through an order. You take orders. That's it.

Later on, if you're strong or lucky, you get a better grip on yourself — you get your common sense back. That's after you're out of boot camp. But you probably never come out of it the same as when you came in.

In some ways, it helped me later. I learned to concentrate better. Fighting that marksmanship thing made me apply myself to details, like the miserable and unforgiving need to hit a target, cut off from all the people and problems and events of your life outside the firing range. On those endless, long marches, you learn to punish yourself and your body just to get it the hell done with. Don't let the other guys down, that sort of stuff.

But, while you learn what your body is capable of, you also get hurt by a conditioning that's not related to any other conditioning in your life. It sure as hell isn't related to playing baseball.

In those six months of pushing myself somebody else's way, the upper part of my body got very tight and strong, the muscles got solid and not as elastic as they should've been, just from doing all those push-ups and chins. You find that they don't help you in baseball. In the marines, you repeat those exercises over and over again; your body changes and you develop differently. I even tried push-ups with my right arm only, and it got real strong, so strong that I could do all sorts of push-ups one-handed.

Then they finally sprung me, and there I was: a graduate guerrilla fighter and trained jungle fighter who could do fifty right-handed push-ups. Sure, when I shoved off and hustled down to spring training in March of 1966, I was able to show off in the clubhouse. The only problem was that there were only two or three weeks left before the start of the new baseball season and the Mets hadn't bothered to tell me that I was supposed to be the left-handed starter on the pitching staff. Later, when you're older and more established, they may tell you *who* you are. But when you're a young kid, they don't. You can do the right-handed push-ups on the locker-room floor, but suddenly you have trouble doing left-handed fastballs from sixty and a half feet away.

So I came back and thought, holy cow, I'm here. Maybe they thought I knew what I was supposed to start doing, but I didn't do it. And couldn't.

I did everything hard right away, throwing the ball too hard too soon and trying to make my muscles forget about six months of training and straining as a pickle. And before long, I felt a stiffness in my left elbow. I didn't want to say anything, I was afraid they wouldn't keep me around if I admitted I had a sore arm. They might even release me and, at the age of twenty-one, I'd be an "ex" everything. So I kept my mouth shut, especially after we opened in New York a few weeks later, and then I pitched a few outings and my arm got worse and worse.

Finally, during a foggy night game late in May, my arm was smarting real bad and I felt that it had snapped or something. I couldn't even throw anymore, and I thought it was completely shot.

Gus Mauch helped me back to the clubhouse, trying to console me by telling me I was too young to take it seriously. But all I kept thinking was how embarrassed I'd be if they sent me home to California after I blew it in New York.

Later, in the trainer's room, they put ice on the elbow and gave me shots in the crazybone area. The doctor looked at the arm and said I had tendonitis: my elbow was inflamed, and I had hardly any sensation in my little finger and ring finger because the swelling and irritation had affected the nerve. I was put on Butazolidin pills, the same stuff they gave Dancer's Image, the horse that had the Kentucky Derby taken away from him, and I had my first sore arm.

Two weeks later, I tried to throw again but still had pain; they put me on the disabled list for a month and only let me throw batting practice. Then they shipped me out to Jacksonville so I could take my time letting the arm heal, and Dr. LaMotte — Peter LaMotte, the Mets orthopedic surgeon — told me I was lucky to be a kid and strong. At least you know how you hurt your arm, he said, there's no mystery about that. I told him the arm had hurt for some time and that I hadn't reported it, and he said, this is your bread and butter, so we've got to hear about it from you — the worst that'll happen when we do

is that you'll go on the disabled list. Maybe you wouldn't
have missed a game if you'd told us you had a problem;
now you've hurt yourself and the club, too.

Just to show you how much I hurt myself that year, I
pitched in fifteen games for the Mets, started twelve of
them and finished only one. I won two and lost nine,
and the guy who keeps the decimal points for the team
says I had an earned run average of 5.37 — that's 5.37
runs off me every nine innings. After they sent me south
to Jacksonville, I started six games, pitched relief in five
others, won two and lost two, and had an E.R.A. of 4.22.
That doesn't win any Nobel Prizes, either.

But I learned something, I guess. I had to be sick to be
healthy. Because the next year, 1967, they kept me at
Jacksonville, and I got myself straightened out pretty
good. Started twenty-one times, went all the way fourteen times, had a ten and nine record and raised a few
eyebrows with my E.R.A., which was 1.99, to be exact.

The year before, the Jacksonville manager was Solly
Hemus and for me the outstanding development was that
I got rid of my bad arm and also saw Tom Seaver pitch
for the first time. A super pitcher, you could tell right
away, big and strong and smart as hell. And then in '67,
the manager was Bill Virdon and the outstanding development was that he talked to me a lot about pitching and
how I should handle myself. Virdon, who later managed
the Pittsburgh Pirates and the Yankees, became a very
important man in helping me to get to know myself. I
didn't know Gil Hodges at the time, but they turned out
to be very much alike.

When the Mets finally called me back at the end of the
season, their manager was Wes Westrum, the club was

still in last place, and he was absorbed by big things — like saving his job. So I noticed that he didn't congratulate me on my year at Jacksonville.

I was in center field one day shagging flies and he called me to second base, where the ball bucket was and where he used to stand watching everything. And he said, we're going to start you in a couple of days. I just want you to know we have rules and regulations around here, so watch yourself and take care of yourself.

I got pissed off and said, "For Christ's sake, Wes, I just had a fairly super year in the minors and you haven't even mentioned that to me yet. I spent the whole year down there trying to contain myself and prepare myself, and before that I spent six months in the marines. Are the rules any different here than down there, or different than they were last spring? What about pitching? Who am I gonna be pitching against? All you talk about is rules and regulations."

He said, "I just wanted you to know how things are around here." And I said, "Okay, I'll see you around." Shit.

When we got out to Los Angeles, he started me in a game and I was doing super — four real strong innings, and I struck out six guys. I was a little wild maybe but I was getting out of trouble with strikeouts. Then in the fifth, I got in a little trouble again. I walked a guy, gave up a base hit, got a guy out, the shortstop booted one, and now the bases were loaded. But I was pitching real good and wasn't losing the game. Still, Westrum took me out, and I sure as hell couldn't understand why.

In the tunnel leading from the field to the locker rooms there was a big water bucket, and I kicked it all the way into the clubhouse. The clubhouse guy, Jimmy, looked at me as if to say: Please don't touch this place, I got it all set up. He had a sad look on his face and all that buffet food spread on tables for after the game, and he was sort of pleading with me, don't tear up all this shit on me, McGraw.

I didn't, but when the game was over, I went in to Wes and asked him what's the story — ever since I came up, you've been giving me a bad time. Now here I was pitching pretty good when I get a couple of bad breaks and you take me out. We're in last place anyway, what are we fighting for — the pennant? You know, I'm not trying to tell you how to manage, just asking you to let me pitch.

I didn't realize it at the time, but "we" were fighting for something after all. His job.

Four or five days later, he gave me another turn at starting and when I went out to the mound after warming up, I knew I didn't have great stuff. And they kicked the shit out of me. Line drives all over the place. It was the Astrodome, and we were lucky just to stay alive. I gave up eight runs in five innings, and this time Wes just wouldn't take me out. He made me stay out there and take it. Just like I'd demanded. But I thought it was horseshit, a sort of you-pop-off, you-take-the-consequences sort of thing.

Another time, a bunch of the guys went out to Disneyland when we were in L.A., and that night we got beat real bad. So Wes announced that Disneyland was off-limits. Get that: Mickey Mouse was off-limits because he made you too tired to play ball, but Joe's Bar was all right. Man, I'm not even sure that six months as a pickle at Parris Island prepared me for that one.

9

Two on a Toboggan

I HAVE A CONFESSION to make, and I hope the Mets front office won't be too upset, because they're hearing it for the first time: When I twisted my ankle during the winter of 1970 after we won the World Series, I didn't slip on the ice taking out the garbage. I sprained it while Ron Swoboda and I were tobogganing down the side of a sump on Long Island.

It was only a couple of years after Dr. LaMotte had given me that little lecture about not hiding sore arms. Well, I didn't hide the twisted ankle. But I did hide the way it happened because it was contract-signing time, and Swoboda and I already had well-deserved reputations for being the two guys most likely to tailspin a toboggan. We didn't think we needed another caper in our credentials.

This happened a couple of months after Swoboda made that hair-raising, tumbling catch that saved the Series game against the Baltimore Orioles. I had a great view of it, because I was sitting in the bullpen. I sat in the bullpen for the whole Series, in fact. But now we had our winner's checks for $18,133 apiece, and my wife

Phyllis and I decided to spend the winter (and some of the check) in New York instead of back home in California.

You have to appreciate the fact that there is a difference in personality between Swoboda and me, even though most people might pair us as strange ones. Rocky is big and sturdy and almost deliberate when he's doing demon things, and he comes at you head-on; I'm more flighty in a way, more unpredictable, more like the hair trigger on a submachine gun.

One thing I owe Swoboda: He taught me how to use chopsticks. Once we were in Milwaukee when they were in the National League, and he took me to a Chinese restaurant and ate with chopsticks. I'd never used them before, so I asked him: "Where in hell did you learn that?" He said his grandfather was Chinese. "Holy shit, you don't look Chinese," I said, and he doesn't. Later, I found out that it was his grandmother's second marriage, so Swoboda had a Chinese step-grandfather. Anyway, since then I've always used chopsticks myself, and if I owe anything in the world to Ron Swoboda, it's that he taught me to use them.

Also, how to sprain my ankle on a toboggan. What happened that time was that Phyllis and I were visiting Swoboda and his wife Cecelia in Syosset on Long Island, and it had been snowing real hard. One of the neighborhood kids had a toboggan, and there was a sump nearby, a big drainage area where excess water filled up an excavation.

Well, this was outstanding. A bunch of kids started playing with us and we would go down the sides of this sump on the toboggan; it was really a great trip. Somebody would push you at the top of the hill and you'd pick up a lot of speed because the sides were steep, like forty-five degrees. At the bottom of the hill, which was maybe forty yards long, you'd level off for about twenty-five yards at the bottom, then you'd hit a little rise, about five feet slanting up at another forty-five-degree angle. This time, when your sled got to the top of the rise, it would shoot off into the air before hitting bottom again.

Swoboda and I got the bright idea that if there were two of us on the sled instead of just one, there'd be more weight and we'd get more momentum to make that jump. Okay, Ron got in front and I got behind him, the kids gave us a good push, and we were flying. We hit that five-foot rise at the bottom and took off, about six or seven feet in the air, and came down ass-over and were spread out all over the place.

"Ron, you okay?" I said, and he felt himself carefully to see if he had broken any bones or anything. "Yeah," he said, "okay. You?" And I did the same, and we seemed okay. We had big shitty grins all over our faces now and we said, let's do it again. This time, I was in front and Swoboda in back, and we hit that rise and flew off again.

When we hit the ground, Swoboda came down right on top of me, all 205 pounds, and my leg got underneath and was twisted as we sprawled all over hell. This time he said, "You okay?" And I said, "No, my ankle. It might be broken."

It wasn't, it was only twisted, but I had to sign my contract for the next season — it had just been mailed out by the Mets — and I sure as hell didn't want to tell them what happened, at least not *how* it happened. Especially since they thought we were nuts in the first place. We didn't want anybody to go around saying, "I told you so."

So I told the club that I had been taking out the garbage and slipped on the icy sidewalk, and they said okay. It was an accident, and it might've happened to anybody. You know, it wasn't like Jim Lonborg of the Boston Red Sox creaming his leg while he was skiing. Not if I hurt my ankle putting out the ever-lovin' garbage.

When we got back to Swoboda's house, we stopped on the doorstep and put on a show to make it look good. We started screaming and hollering as if I'd just slipped on the ice there; not even our wives knew, we were too embarrassed to tell them. They thought I slipped in front of his door, and it was two or three months before I even told Phyllis what the hell had happened.

It's one thing to hurt yourself on your own time in your own damn-fool way; you never get any sympathy. But if you get hurt in the trenches, they really do it up big. Pete LaMotte is a calm, cool guy and he'll scare you sometimes with his casualness about injuries. He diagnoses them rapidly and you wonder if he really understands what you're saying. But he gets it right away.

I don't think the doctor or the trainer, whether it was Gus Mauch or Tommy McKenna and Joe Deer later, ever allowed us to take a prescription drug. They had a real tough policy that way. I know you hear rumbles about this subject now, and I don't know anything about what football teams do. But I do know that LaMotte hates to prescribe *anything* unless it's absolutely necessary.

Some of the guys, I've seen a few, sometimes take a greenie every now and then. But I never saw people on our team relying on them. Not on the Mets. Greenies are amphetamines, and they're not for a hangover, if that's what you're thinking. A guy might slip one if he feels slow, but he'll be pretty secret about it if he does.

In '66 or '67, we had a second baseman at Jacksonville who took greenies quite a bit. Once, just for the hell of it, I tried one of them. This must be my day for confessions. It just made me real talkative, that's all — if anybody can tell the difference between when I'm talkative and when I'm real talkative.

Anyway, this guy liked to have a lot of fun, and he never could find enough time to sleep. What hurt him most in baseball was the thing that's most dangerous to do: he got to the point where he'd take a greenie to get "up" for a game and, later, a sleeping pill to get back down so he could sleep.

But all the greenie did for me was to make me talkative, and very active on the bench. When I was pitching, though, I found that I wasn't thinking much about the hitters — I just kept taking the ball from the catcher and throwing it back. I pitched eight innings that way and all of a sudden in the ninth, I had nothing left. We lost, 2 to 1. Without the greenie, I would've stayed in. I always get keyed up for games anyway. I haven't taken another one since.

I tried marijuana once, too, but it was in the dead of winter in Vietnam in 1969, right after the Mets won the World Series. The commissioner's office put together two trips to the Far East so ballplayers could visit GI's. They had Joe DiMaggio and Swoboda on the first trip, and me and Pete Ward, Ron Taylor, Denny McLain, and Bob Elson, the broadcaster, in the other one.

We'd bounce around to little fire bases that the big shows never reached. We'd spend all day in copters, jump out, and toss a football or drink a beer. Then in the evening, we'd visit the hospitals.

It got heavy after a while because we'd seen a lot but could absorb just so much. And it was a controversial war, besides.

One night in Saigon, a couple of enlisted men were assigned to show us around, and they took me up on the roof of the hotel where the military people kept the USO and showed movies. I figured that if I was ever going to try smoking marijuana, this was as private a spot as any. It was one o'clock in the morning, a clear night, the sky filled with copter patrols. You could hear and see the war out there.

They had this Vietnam grass, and it shook me up right away. It made me start to laugh, as though I was in the middle of a film about the war and not on the roof of the building surrounded by the real war. I was sure that any minute John Wayne would come charging over.

Even when we went downstairs, I was weird and laughing, and not too polite to people. I went over to Ron Taylor, who was having a serious talk with two other persons. Ron was a few years older than me and he'd pitched in the World Series for the St. Louis Cardinals before the Mets got him, and he told me to butt out because I was interrupting him and acting strange.

He got the notion I was high and he knew it wasn't from liquor, so he finally came over and slapped my face. I was stunned, but I got the idea and left.

The next day, I apologized to Ron and he apologized to me. We talked about it a while, too. He'd studied drugs and knew a lot about them. In fact, after he retired from baseball, he decided to go to medical school, even though he already was an electrical engineer — and he made it. Anyway, it was my first and last tiff with pot.

Look, I'm naturally up anyway, I don't need any help. Remember, after my first game in the bigs, they had to give me a tranquilizer to calm me down, and the same before my first start in Chicago. Just for me to pitch the way I want to, and to be effective, I have to be keyed up and nervous — the juices have to flow.

Baseball itself is a high for me, and Bowie Kuhn doesn't write my speeches. Don't forget, we did all kinds of things to fatten me up so I *could* have a shot at the pros. In junior college, I used to drive home for lunch every day and Dad always had a hot meal waiting, barbecued chicken or spaghetti. Then I'd stop across the street for a milk shake. I only had two years to get big. I weighed 140 when I graduated from high school and 160 two years later.

So I got kicks out of just being in pro ball. It's a hell of a way to make your living. That's another reason I'd do a lot of crazy things on the mound. I was naturally high — and I was also unsure of myself. Every time I'd get into a key situation and would get a strike, I'd raise my arms or my hands and go a little crazy. Casey used to say that I'd watch the first baseman and second baseman chase a ground ball to the right side and would forget to cover first base myself because I was so absorbed in watching them make a great play. Then if the guy got on, I might kick the rubber, holler at the umpire, or just generally get pissed off.

I remember the first game that I pitched after I came back to the bigs in '67. They didn't leave me in too long.

But the next start was very important to me. It was against the Philadelphia Phillies. Those guys used to get on me all the time, so it was another of those things that made me self-conscious. That day, I still didn't know how strong my arm was or how hard I could throw, but I ended up pitching a two-hitter, only giving up two singles, and we won, 5 to 1.

The game ended when Cleon Jones made a leaping catch off the scoreboard in right-center on a ball that Johnny Callison hit. It was a super catch, and as soon as he made it I started jumping up and down. Even the New York *Times* wrote that "the effervescent McGraw threw his glove into the air when Cleon Jones registered the final out of the day with a leaping catch, depriving Callison of an extra-base hit."

The *Times* also reported, for history I guess, that it was our fifty-fifth victory, the most ever for the Mets in one season at that time. But I didn't care too much about that. I was just going off in all directions because I'd pitched nine innings after a sore elbow. Jerry Grote was the catcher and he ran out to the mound. But instead of shaking hands, I jumped in his arms, and everybody thought I was nuts.

The next day, the manager of the Phillies, Gene Mauch, really ripped me. He said I was immature and he wouldn't want a player like me on his team. But I notice now that he's running the Montreal club he greatly admires that same quality in Tim Foli. He just didn't like it on a guy on the other team. Hell, it was a milestone for me. I'd just beaten Jim Bunning, a damned fine pitcher, and it showed me I could pitch in the big leagues after hurting my arm. Everybody else in the world can't understand that, I guess. Gene Mauch can't. I guess he didn't know me very well.

At the end of the 1967 season, and this will probably be good news to Gene Mauch, something happened that quieted me down a bit: I met and married Phyllis Kline, and after that it wasn't me alone anymore. I had a wife sitting out there in the stands, too, and I didn't want her to be embarrassed by my jerk act, so I decided to try to cut out the screwball stuff.

Just to show you how dignified and mature marriage made me, I'll let her tell you in her own words how we got together, because it's not the sort of subject where I should be editorializing. Okay, Phyl, you're on:

Well, it was the winter of 1967, right around New Year's of 1968. I was what they called Number 3 on the transfer list at TWA, where I was a stewardess. It meant I wanted to be transferred from New York back home to California, and I was third from the top for transfer. So I didn't want to miss the phone call from the office with the good news.

I was going with a guy on the Coast, anyway, and this time my roommates and girl friends were going out for a bite to eat and they coaxed me to go with them. We went to a place on the East Side called Mister Laffs, it was run by Phil Linz, who used to play for the Yankees, and apparently a lot of football and baseball players would go there, and that's where I met Tug that evening.

He was pretty drunk when I met him. He said he played baseball, and honestly, I didn't know you could make your living playing baseball. I just didn't know you could make a living playing sports at all. He really seemed flaky and flighty, immature, and I didn't like him too much. After all, I already had this boyfriend back home and I wanted to go home to my family and friends. But right away, that night Tug told me he was going to marry me.

In spite of the way he came on, it turned out to be the nicest evening I'd had in a long time. The next spring, I went to St. Pete with my girl friend, who lived there, but I was afraid Tug would keep pestering me. And he did. He kept asking me to marry him. But he was really trying to be nice, and one night at a place called Ted's Hideaway, we were there with Ron and Cecelia Swoboda. They were dancing and we were sitting there, and I just said, "Yes." He said, "Yes, what." I nearly blew my mind.

Now to go back and do justice to him: that day we first met, Tug must've had a bad time at the barber school on the Bowery where he was developing his "sideline." Somebody really gave him a hard time. This man was on welfare and he went in for a free haircut, and his problems really got to Tug, that's the way he is. Tug got him looking like a banker, then went to Mr. Laffs and got buzzed.

Thank you, Mrs. McGraw. Now I'll give you credit for naming the dog I brought home from the barber school: Poochie is what we called her, but you said to spell it Pucci and "give her a little class." Check.

I suppose I can't just say "barber school" and let it go at that, as though every red-blooded guy in town attended one at some time or other. Well, there was a method to my madness: My dad always cut our hair when we were kids, and one day I remember asking him to let me try giving him a trim. He said okay, and after that I started earning pocket money in high school and college cutting other kids' hair.

Before I met Phyllis that winter in New York, my barber down in the Financial District steered me to the Tri-City Barber School because I kept talking about developing a sideline in case baseball didn't pan out for me. It was down on the Bowery and I became a real dedicated student.

I also became shook-up, because these guys would come in and they'd be in real bad shape. They'd fall asleep when you gave them a hot towel, things like that. They didn't come in for a haircut so much as to get cleaned up and sobered up when they went to collect their government checks. They'd come in with layers of dirt sometimes, and layers of hair. Once I even used Ajax cleanser to spruce up a guy who was especially raunchy.

Another time a guy came in who needed help desperately. I worked on him all morning, styled his hair, gave him a Clark Gable mustache and a facial, and got him looking pretty great. Then he went down and picked up his disability check, returned, and gave me a twenty-five-cent tip. It was his pride coming back, and tipping the barber was part of it.

We were supposed to charge them fifty cents, but most times I didn't. I just listened to their stories — how they had lost it all, or how they'd get it back someday. I got so wrapped up in it that I hardly missed a day all winter. And by the time I met Phyllis that night, I was close to getting my license as an apprentice barber — and an expert listener.

When I went to spring training that year, I took two things with me from the school: my "rating" and my dog. Bringing Pucci down to St. Pete seemed like a neat idea to me, especially when I'd drive him out to Huggins–Stengel Field every morning and tie him up in the little patio outside the cottage where Johnny Murphy and our other staff executives had their offices. It was a nice little walkway with a picket fence and some flower beds, and somebody decided to call it "Payson Place" after the owner of the club, Joan Payson.

But Pucci got me into the doghouse by digging up the flowers outside Murphy's door. Then, they wouldn't let me throw the screwball, so I had a bad spring with the team, too. Still, I survived until the final "cut" late in March. One night I was cooking steak in my room at the Colonial Inn when a sportswriter called and asked if I thought I'd make the team on the basis of my previous season or be dropped on the basis of this spring.

While we were talking on the phone, the steak caught fire in the pan. So I opened the door to air the joint out, and Pucci wandered out. She trotted down the corridor to the room where Dick Selma and Danny Frisella were living. They were having a "party" at the time, trying to drown out the world because Selma had made the club but Frisella hadn't.

So they sort of boozed old Pucci up, feeding her a few nips. It must have upset her a little because she left a load right in front of Joe Pignatano's room. Then, Piggy came out of his room in his bare feet to see what the commotion was, and naturally he stepped smack into Pucci's deposit.

Man, he put up a frightening Italian clamor, complete with cussing and howling, the way only a coach can. And the next day, for probably the best of reasons, I got sent to Jacksonville — with my dog. And that's where we were when Phyllis arrived to join my traveling circus.

We were married in Jacksonville, because that's where the Mets assigned me at the beginning of the 1968 season. The Mets had Jerry Koosman as their big left-handed pitcher and Gil Hodges as their new manager, and I didn't show them much in spring training. So my screwball and myself were given a ticket to Jacksonville, and Phyllis and I got married early one Saturday morning before a double-header.

We had a coffee-and-tea reception before the games, and a bourbon-and-Scotch reception after them. They had this circus tent down the right-field line at the ball park where they served buffet dinners during games, and after we got done playing Columbus that day, we had the guys and their wives over for the handshakes. The hell of it was that I was supposed to pitch the next day and Clyde McCullough, the manager, decided to have a little horseplay. When we were leaving, he gave Phyllis the thumbs-down sign. She was just learning about baseball and took everything very strictly. To be perfectly honest about it, I wanted to hop into the sack. But she took Mc-Cullough's nonsense literally: you got to pitch, so . . . well, don't.

It got to be a family joke: every time we thought we'd sneak in our honeymoon after that something kept getting in the way. After the Sunday game the weekend we got married, the club left on a road trip, so Phyl became a baseball widow fast. Then, at the end of the season, my brother Hank was up in Williamsport and he hadn't even met her yet. I had a new Pontiac Grand Prix and we decided to drive home to the Coast, see Hank on the way, and also have our honeymoon besides.

Well, that scheme got botched because Hank hurt himself fairly badly in one of their last games. There were two outs and he was on first base in the first inning. The next batter hit a ground ball to second, and the second baseman came over to field it and was standing in the base path when Hank went running past. Hank tried to avoid him and sort of jumped over him, but came down on the base of his head and jackknifed over. They came out to see if he was okay, and he stayed in the game as the centerfielder. He thought he was having gas pains, so the trainer gave him some Pepto-Bismol. But the next inning the pain got worse, and in the fifth, Hank just doubled up and collapsed.

A doctor happened to be in the stands watching, and he came down to the clubhouse and asked if he could see the injured player. He examined Hank, thought it might be his appendix, and sent him to the hospital. But nobody seemed to be in too much of a hurry, and the blood test there didn't show any high count of white cells; his pulse was in the seventies. They didn't know that he had a highly "athletic" heart with a normal pulse rate in the forties, and he was nearly twice that.

The doctor still thought it was appendicitis and said they should operate fairly soon. He said he could do it himself that night, but would wait until the next day if Hank wanted to call Dad. Hank said let's do it now and call Dad tomorrow. So they operated and the blood came rushing out. He'd ruptured a vessel and had already lost almost the maximum amount of blood that a person can; the doctor said he'd have bled to death internally if they hadn't operated within the hour.

The next day, Phyllis and I left Florida in the car and drove to Pennsylvania, where Hank was in the hospital. He wasn't ready to fly yet and was still nervous from the operation besides, so we picked him up and started for

California. And that shot our honeymoon, too: Phyl and the dog were in the back, my brother and I in the front. The first hotel stop we made was in Cheyenne, Wyoming.

When we got home, we bought a pickup truck with a camper, which we took to spring training the next year. By then, Phyl wanted to know all about my family, especially my mother, whom she hadn't met. So I took her down to Hayward, where my mother was living at the time, and Phyl's heart went out to her. She just felt sad that this woman was split from her family and couldn't be closer to her three sons. On top of that, my mother's second husband had died a few months before, so Phyllis got the idea of inviting her to spring training with us in the camper. The drive there was now supposed to be our honeymoon at long last. But that time, my mother was with us, courtesy of my wife. Also friend dog.

As it turned out, we accomplished a lot, and Phyllis did it. When I finally got down to work in St. Pete that spring, things started falling into place. The year before, Hodges hadn't liked what he saw and I just didn't make the team, but in '69, I not only escaped the expansion draft but found that me and my screwjie were welcome in camp. Koosman and a big rookie named Les Rohr were there, along with several other guys looking for work as left-handed pitchers, and the Mets honestly didn't know what was in store for me. But they let me throw the screwball. Then they decided they had no vacancy for a starter but did have one for a relief pitcher, and McGraw snapped it up.

What happened was that Hodges told me I had two choices: go down to the minors again as a starting pitcher or try to make it with the Mets as a reliever. The main idea is to play in the big leagues, so I didn't wrestle with that one too long. I guess if you wait long enough, you outgrow your problems. Like my old phobia about pitching to the same line-up the third time around — when they'd pounce on you because by then you were becoming old hat. Well, in my new job, I usually faced guys only once. And so I had a new wife, a new job, a new specialty, and a new "office" down the right-field line in the Shea bullpen.

I even came up with a new system to rate myself. It was sort of forced on me because nobody seemed to have any idea how to measure a relief pitcher's value. When they sent me my contract in 1970, for example, I found out some interesting things. Like they felt your earned run average wasn't the most important statistic, because it didn't show how many runs were on base when you came into a game. (Those runs, if they scored, were charged against the pitcher who put them on base. So you might get socked around and let in a few runs right off the bat, without any runs being charged against you.) Also, they weren't too impressed with the "save" rule, and neither was I. All you had to do was get into a game, even a 20 to 1 game, and not blow it, and you'd get credit for saving it.

They didn't think too much of that either. Or wins, either, because they figured you just had to be lucky and be in the right place at the right time to pick up a win as a relief pitcher. So those statistics were out the window, too. And I don't know what the hell that *left* for a yardstick.

So I came up with my own system for relief pitchers: my plus and minus system. It reinforces the other statistics that they don't think are too important. What happens is: If there are men on base who "belong" to the previous pitcher, you count each man on base as a plus if he doesn't score off you. If one scores, it's a minus, even though the other pitcher put him on. If I gave up a hit and two runs scored, two minuses for McGraw.

You keep track of your pluses and minuses, and at the end of the year you figure a percentage out of it, just like a won-and-lost percentage. It should come out somewhere around .700 to be really outstanding. Then when the general manager leans across the desk and says, "We're not interested in your E.R.A. because you're a relief pitcher," you'll have some kind of answer.

I've talked to a bunch of guys about it. When Danny Frisella was with the Mets, he used to keep track of himself with my system. Clay Carroll and Jim Brewer think it's okay, and I rapped with Sparky Lyle about it, too. It's a new ball game these days. Fewer runs are scored because of better defense and pitching, and there's more pinch-hitting and platooning — all of which comes down to a need for more relief pitching. You need a bullpen to keep you in the close games, and relief pitching's become sort of the super-tenth position.

Anyway, that's the way I try to turn the conversation when I'm in there talking money with the man. I know Seaver is supposed to go in with all kinds of stats and answers. And I do now, too. I know a guy named Al Lewbell, who owns Clive Jewelers on Madison Avenue in New York — Swoboda knew him first and introduced me to him. Alvin has pretty good expertise in law, he discusses the selling points and the weak points with me, and advises me on a lot of things — like the best possible salary figure that would be fair to me and the ball club, too. He also knows what makes the city tick, and I'm a guy from a small town. But at contract time, Alvin has two young boys who like sports and they get together all the stats on my pitching, all my ammunition — plus and minus McGraw.

Sometimes when I'm pitching in a royal mess, I think of my plus and minus signs as though they are little people chasing me into Bob Scheffing's office while he and I are sparring over money. Then I wish to hell I'd never gotten so damned analytical. Like one day in Wrigley Field in 1971. It was our first visit into Chicago late in April and we'd finished third the year before after winning the pennant in 1969.

Now it's the tenth inning and the Cubs have the bases loaded with one out. The Chicago Cubs are real bastards with bats in their hands, and we had a sort of old-fashioned thing going with them even before we knocked them out of first place in '69 after they had a thirteen-and-a-half-game lead on us in the middle of August.

This day, the lead in the game changed sides four times, and now it was all tied at six apiece in the bottom of the tenth. I'd come into the game in the seventh to replace Ron Taylor after he went out for a pinch hitter. And in each of the last three innings before the tenth, I'd let at least one guy get on base. That's me: I live dangerously. Except now in the tenth, I went too far. Jim Hickman opened with a base hit, then I missed a 3-and-2 pitch on Hal Breeden for a walk. So Don Kessinger laid down a perfect sacrifice bunt, and they had two guys on second and third.

Now Ken Rudolph's up, and I'm being real careful.

Our infield's pulled in, and we don't want to put him on because then I'll have no base open and might walk in the winning run. But I tried to be too cute, and I missed with my breaking stuff and was too low with a fastball. Ball four, and they're loaded.

The tip that I was nervous came when Duffy Dyer headed out to the mound, making one of a catcher's favorite speeches: "You're guiding the ball." And out of the corner of my eye, I could see we were going to have company pretty soon — Gil was walking out in his deliberate way, one little step after another, taking his time, his hands in his back pockets.

Usually Gil didn't take the trip himself unless he wanted to change pitchers, and I knew we had a guy heating up in the bullpen. When he reached us, he was all Hodges: calm, relaxed, no sign of emotion. "How do you feel?" McGraw: "I feel fine. I'm not tired, but Duffy says I'm guiding the ball and not throwing it."

Now we had more company. Harrelson from short, Donn Clendenon from first, the umpire from behind the plate, who was trying to hustle us the hell out of there. But Gil never hurried. "I agree with Duff," he said, as though we were out there talking about two other guys and Chicago didn't have the bases loaded with one out in the tenth. "So if you're not tired," Gil said, getting the message through, "wind up and throw the ball."

That meant one thing to me, man: he wasn't going to yank me. And I started to build up energy and nerves, just like he'd slipped me a can of spinach and I pulled a Popeye. While I was congratulating myself, Gil walked over and told Harrelson to move the outfield in a few yards, and then something happened that made me blow my mind. The umpire, with his copy of the line-up in one hand and a pencil in the other, called to Gil: "You mean you're not gonna make a change?"

Damn, but I wished I hadn't heard him say that, because it meant he thought Gil was nuts for leaving me in. So I got infuriated with the umpire for second-guessing the manager.

Then, while I stood there staring him down and trying to pull myself together again, I could hear applause and screams and roars all over the place, and I couldn't figure out what the hell was happening. Then I looked over to the Cubs dugout and saw Ernie Banks choosing a bat in the rack. Beautiful.

What I wanted to do was make him hit the ball on the ground and hope for the double play: I had to go with my screwjie all the way, if I could. But I missed the outside with the first two and was behind two-and-o. Banks had the eyes of an eagle and he wouldn't bite on just anything. My problem now was, two more balls and I'd force in the winning run, so I had to throw the fastball. And praise the Lord, old Leo Durocher had the "take" on and Ernie took.

Now it was two-and-one and he wouldn't be taking anymore, so back to the screwjie I went. I took a big deep breath to get the weight off my chest, and I thought back how Dad used to tell me to do that when I was a kid, and I thought "thank you" for the breath. Then I threw two screwjies in a row for swinging strikes, and Ernie's gone.

Now they've got a kid named Jose Ortiz up there, a kid who can hit — he hit .308 at Tucson before they called him up. And I worked him up to one ball and two strikes, and then threw a superscrewball that started right at his shoulder, making him quit on it, and then broke down into Duffy's mitt, right across the plate, I thought. Ball two, the umpire said. The umpire with the line-up card and the itchy pencil.

Now I was ready to blow my stack. I mean smoke coming out my ears and my jugular vein popping out to there and my face all red and hot. You know, the inning should've been over, but wasn't, and now I was on the verge of a full-fledged tantrum. So I turned around to center field before I had a chance to pop off and say anything he'd make me regret. I even walked to the back of the mound, bent over, and made like I was tying my shoelace. It wasn't untied, but I was coming undone and needed the time to cool off.

Whatever I'd throw next, I knew one thing: I'd have the same guy calling the pitch. Also, the count was two-and-two now, and nothing on earth was going to change that. I also knew that everybody in the park, from the guy in the last row to Durocher, knew I'd probably deal him another screwball. But Duffy and I must've been on the same wavelength because he squatted and gave me the sign: fastball low and away. And I fired.

Jose must've been looking for the screwjie, too, because he watched it snap in there straight as an arrow, and even friend umpire didn't argue. He threw his right hand straight up in the air with the fist tight, and I was out of the inning.

When I got into the dugout, I was shaking like hell all over, and I'd had it, really had had it. Gil thought so, too, because he came over and just patted me on the ass and said: "Nice going, that's all for today."

Then he sent Nolan Ryan in and for the next two

innings Nollie blew them away with his hard stuff and we won it in the twelfth, 7 to 6. I don't remember getting dressed or getting on the bus or taking the elevator up to my room or anything. Only that I was trembling and flashing back in my mind to all kinds of things, and plus and minus signs coming out of the woodwork like little people. And reaching over to the night table for the jug of Irish.

10

I'm a People and I'm Screwed Up

THE PEOPLE who meant the most to me in my life were probably my brother Hank, who was suspended from baseball because his hair was too long; my mother and father, who were divorced while I was growing up, and Gil Hodges, who died while he was my boss at the age of forty-seven.

It was on Easter Sunday in 1972 that he played twenty-seven holes of golf with his coaching staff and then collapsed from a massive heart attack. It happened in West Palm Beach a couple of days after the 600 players in the big leagues had voted to go on strike.

Suddenly, the new baseball season was delayed, we were all caught in a bitter fight with the owners, and during it we guys on the Mets attended the funeral of the man who had made us aware of responsibility and respect and discipline. I was twenty-six years old, and I felt stranded.

When Gil was running the ball club, you always felt that things were sane, even if you were kind of insane, the way I felt during the spring of 1970. There never was a time when he meant more to me. Hodges was a man of few words — all of them effective. Sometimes he would just look at you and deliver the message. Other times, he would put it on the line in a fairly long bit of rapping, one on one. There were even times when he'd watch me pull one of my stunts and say nothing.

When the year opened, the Mets were riding high. We had just won the World Series against Baltimore and the banquet circuit was so heavy that winter that Phyllis and I stayed in New York so I could make as many appearances as possible. Then in February we headed south for spring training. The club was shaping up with everybody signed to contracts and lots of money scattered around, and then the city of St. Pete decided to welcome us to camp with a "day" for the Mets. They called the city something like Metsville for one day, they scheduled a big parade down Central Avenue, and they held a dinner for us that night in the big new Bayside Center down the block from Al Lang Field.

Well, the parade got rained out, which was in keeping with our tradition in baseball. But the dinner went off okay — the place was filled and they had all the ballplayers on a big stage with the dinner tables down in the arena where basketball and hockey games were usually played. The mayor was there and so was Governor Claude Kirk.

The dinner went fine and everybody made speeches. Then it came time for the governor to give his talk, and he started rambling on about the Mets and America, and how young people today let their hair grow and never bathe and are irresponsible and never care for the future of the country. Then he turned around toward us guys on the ball club and said, now here's a fine bunch with short hair and ties and coats and clean shirts and no dirt behind their ears, so to speak. If every kid in America could be like this, he said, our country wouldn't have any problems.

He was aiming his speech at an audience of mainly elderly people, who grew up when everybody wore coats and ties and had short hair. And he was using us as a prop. It really bugged me because most of the players there were individuals, in talent and personal style. Sure, because of a dress code that Hodges had on the club, you'd have to wear coats and ties on the road and at dinner. But I know 99 percent of the guys would rather not have worn them and been more comfortable. Most of the guys would've preferred to let their hair grow longer, too, but didn't want any problems with the front office. So the hair generally was shorter then — the sideburns were starting to creep down, but Governor Kirk didn't mention them.

Look, we felt we were just as concerned about problems in the country as anybody, and we could dress the way we pleased without losing any of that concern. Players today do have longer hair and dress more casually because they're young and they're in step with the times. But Kirk was trying to make an example of us for his own benefit, and none of us appreciated it.

When it came time for the players to get awards after dinner, they had a platform set up in the middle of the arena, with tables on all sides and with our Met broadcasters — Lindsey Nelson, Ralph Kiner, and Bob Murphy — announcing us. They'd call your name and you'd go from the dais to the platform and then back.

While you were doing it they'd announce your stats and give a little intro and a fill-in, and everybody would give a lot of applause.

You were supposed to shake hands and say "thank you." But I was still pissed off; no kidding, Kirk's speech had ruined the night for me. Well, one of the big things going around then, and it had been real popular for a couple of years, came out of the Vietnam war — the old Churchill V-for-victory sign. Except now it had become the peace sign, the sign of the dove. And, as I received my award and everybody applauded, I turned around and faced Governor Kirk and gave him the peace sign.

The next day, it caused all kinds of hell. Writers from national magazines and newspapers and television crews were clamoring around me. And it was the first time that I realized that when you're on a championship team, everything you say or do influences a lot of people. But it was the only way I could fight back at Governor Kirk. It was my way of telling people we weren't All-American boys the way he made us out, and that I'd rather speak out for myself and not let other people speak for me, especially for their personal gains.

It was also the wrong time for anybody to go giving any lectures to me about my life-style, or anybody else's. My brother was trying to make the big leagues again that spring with a team that needed help, the Philadelphia Phillies, but he got canned because he was a rebel and wouldn't get his hair cut. My parents crossed paths one day in my hotel room in San Francisco and we had a real disaster. And the shootings at Kent State happened that spring, which made the least sense of all. This all happened in the space of a few weeks, and I don't remember any series of events that ever racked me up so painfully.

My parents — who the hell knows why parents get divorced. It was a medical thing maybe. My mother had been sick, and she got to the point where she was drinking heavily. Then, after the split-up, she remarried, but later the guy she married died of a heart attack. So she had another setback.

Meanwhile, the Mets were working their way along the West Coast and it was supposed to be a happy visit for me. My old grammar school in Vallejo invited me back to speak to the kids, all my friends were going to watch me pitch in Candlestick Park, and my mother and father were supposed to meet me during that weekend — separately.

My happy time started to turn bad, though, in one of our first games on the Coast. I had a problem with Gil. Or, to be more truthful, Gil had a problem with me.

When he called me into the game, there were men on second and third and it was a real mess. So I started out by motioning to the shortstop, who was Teddy Martinez that day. He was a rookie from the Dominican Republic who didn't speak much English, and he was pretty tense anyway. I wanted to put on a pick-off play; you know, give Teddy a sign and try to pick the guy off second. But he said something that sounded like "no comprendo." Then he went back to his position but, before I could pitch, Hodges came out from the dugout and wanted to know what I'd been talking to Martinez about.

I told him I was trying to put on a pick-off. And boy, he really flipped his lid. It's a trick play, I said. Trick play, my foot, he said with real quiet heat. You've got a rookie shortstop who doesn't speak English, you're trying to set up a play we didn't practice, it's a close game, and you're not even worried about getting the hitter out yet. How, he demanded, are you going to get this hitter out? Then, without waiting for me to answer, he said that if we didn't win this game, it would be my ass.

So I stopped fooling around with tricky plays and worked on the hitter. And after we finally won the game, I was sitting in my locker sort of sobbing — you couldn't tell if I was laughing or crying. While this was going on, my dad came to the locker-room door, but I told them not to let him in. I was too embarrassed and mixed up. And it always seemed that I had something to prove whenever we played before my relatives and friends in California, and all I'd proved this time was how stupid and riled-up I could be.

A couple of days later, I arranged this party in my hotel room for my father and the relatives on his side of the family, and people from my old high school. It was after a Saturday game, and the idea was that I'd get together with my mom after the Sunday game the next afternoon. My parents just didn't mix well anymore, and I even had to be careful when I left tickets for them that Dad would be sitting behind third base and Mom behind first base.

So we were all up in the room at the Palace. It was actually a small suite that Ed Kranepool and I had taken, with me paying the difference between that and the double room that they usually put the players in. This time, while my father and his friends were upstairs with Krane and me, my mother showed up at the hotel and was sitting in the lounge having a drink. Several of the coaches were in there, and I didn't want her to end up being embarrassed sitting alone, so I asked her to come up to the room. I had no choice really but to invite her up.

But it was touchy, because she and Dad were always at odds, and you could always feel it in the air that they just didn't get along anymore.

To make things worse, my father had his girl friend and her mother there that day. But when Mom came into the room, they both knew other people were there, so they played it cool for a while. Then Dad's lady friend and her mother went into the next room to get ready to leave, so Mom went over and sat down next to Dad, and I knew that if she sat there long enough, the shit would hit the fan.

I went around and quietly told everybody the party was over, thank you for coming, we were going to start breaking it up now. You know, we have a ball game tomorrow, there's a team curfew, blah-blah-blah. But my mother wasn't paying attention when I went around the room, and she got the idea that she was the first one being asked to leave because she was drinking too much and the party would go on after she left. So she got all shook up and started asking me things like, how come your father isn't leaving and so on. I tried to explain all over again that it was just time for the party to break up and that she wasn't the only one being asked to leave.

Just then, my dad's friend and her mother came out of the ladies' room off the bedroom and they saw I was having trouble with my mother, trying to get her to understand. So they tried to help me: Now, Mabel, Tug's got a day game tomorrow and is trying to get us to go home, etc. And: if you really love your son and want him to pitch well tomorrow and do his job, you'll leave, too.

Well, that was the last straw. Now Mom got infuriated and all of a sudden threw a haymaker from right field, a hook out of nowhere that caught the friend across the jaw. And that started a real brawl in the bedroom.

Mom's about 5-6 and weighs 180, and those two women together didn't weigh that much. The elderly one said something like "You can't treat my daughter like that." And Mom was getting hysterical and the three of them were mixing it up. I was scared that my dad would get into it and things would really get out of control. So I got hold of Kranepool and said, "Don't let Dad in here," because he didn't realize yet what was going on.

Krane was great. He hustled over to Dad and said, "Big Mac, let's have another drink," and started shooting the shit with him in the living room while I was trying to straighten things out in the bedroom. I finally did and I got them out of there. But after I got Mom downstairs into a taxicab, I got all bothered and depressed and worrying, hell, I wonder if this runs in the family. Maybe I was cracking up.

So I went back and finished half a bottle of Irish. And a couple of hours later, they had a room check, and Joe Pignatano came in. Our room looked like a tornado had hit. "What the hell's going on here?" Pig said. I told him we had a party, and Joe just shook his head and walked out.

The next afternoon at Candlestick, I couldn't think or do anything. Just stood and leaned against the outfield fence. When Rube Walker got the pitchers together for our running drill, I took a raincheck. I figured that if I was shot then, I'd better save whatever I had left for the game. But I was so upset I was reeling, and I was praying they wouldn't use me. The hell of it was that in Candlestick the bullpen is out in the open alongside the box seats, so you can't even fall asleep if you want to.

I almost got away with it. But when you're on a losing streak, whether it's you personally or the ball club, nothing seems to go right. This time, Gary Gentry was pitching a good game and had a 5 to 2 lead in the eighth, and then Willie Mays led off for the Giants by ripping one into the seats. That pissed Gary off. He immediately gave up a couple of singles and he was gone.

But Hodges called for Danny Frisella first, which gave me a bit of a reprieve. The only trouble with that, though, was that Frisbee sometimes had problems adjusting to the mound — it was higher than the one in the bullpen and it slopes more; relief pitchers always have trouble adjusting. So the next thing you know, Frisella gives up a run and Hodges is telephoning the bullpen with this: "Get McGraw up." I still couldn't believe it, couldn't believe I'd have to do anything, I felt so shitty. But they got the bases loaded with one out, and the score now was 5 to 4, and in comes McGraw.

I was so nauseous and tight that I couldn't even pick up the catcher's signs, even though I was staring in at him as hard as I could without falling off the mound. Over behind our dugout on the third-base side, I could almost "feel" my dad and his friends and all my old pals from Vallejo. They were all there screaming and yelling at me. Then I fidgeted around, found the mound all strange the way it had been for Frisella, pitched ball one to Fran Healy, and finally decided I was so hung that I didn't give a shit about anything.

So I fiddled around with my stride, shortened it about

five inches as though we were practicing our moves on some playground — and flipped Healy a screwball that he fouled off to Jerry Grote. Then Bobby Bonds struck out on three pitches. In the ninth, Chris Speier flied out to right, Willie Mays looped a little single past shortstop (I settled for that without any argument), Tito Fuentes and Dick Dietz fished for screwballs, and I wobbled into the clubhouse. I got the hell out of sight somewhere in a corner and started sobbing again.

But the thing that happened *off* the field that hurt me the most *on* the field that spring was Kent State. Whatever happens to me at home, I can usually arrange things in my mind sooner or later and get my work done. Most times I can even do it without losing the fun — maybe zest is a better word — that I get out of playing ball. Except when I have a combination of emotional and physical pains the way I did that weekend in San Francisco. But the one thing I never was able to shut off in my mind, or even to explain to myself, was Kent State.

I hadn't been out of the marines all that long myself, and they used to give us classes in riot training. But I never thought it would come to that, even if our unit was ever activated.

These guys in the Ohio National Guard were no different from me and my teammates, and yet other guys were being shot by them — it was that simple and cruel. When we heard the news, there was no way to absorb it and still go on doing the usual routine. I never could believe that the country had reached the point where National Guard guys would have to shoot other people.

You've got to think back and remember the impact of it, if you suspect that I tend to exaggerate things like my own emotions. But I couldn't get myself to go to the ball park and enjoy myself, for God's sake, playing a game of baseball. It didn't seem fair that I could be happy or even safe after the Guard had been called out and started shooting at students at a college. And those guys in the uniforms didn't want any more part of what happened than the students did. But it happened, and I went right in and told Hodges that I couldn't function, couldn't do it, I was blown out of my mind.

Don't ask me why I picked on Hodges, but I did. All the guys in the locker room were upset, and they talked it over and nobody had any answers. So I went in to Gil, not so much because he was the boss but because he was the real strength of the outfit, physically and morally sort of immovable. And that was one of those times when he opened up and did a lot of talking.

Listen, he said, I was in the service, too. I was younger and it was a different situation, a hell of a lot more clear-cut. Now the only thing I can tell you, or tell myself, is that life can be bitter, the way it is today. Adversity comes and goes, bitterness comes and goes. But the thing that stays is your commitment to what's right. Think of where it all starts — your family and your sense of right and wrong, even your job, if it's good. If you let the worst in us ruin the best in us, you'll never find the answer. We'll look for it together, no matter how much we want to cry over the question.

It was a bad time, and Hodges was as affected by it as I was. But he was sweet to me, gentle and sort of fatherly, and I could see that he didn't know exactly what to say either. But he kept the door shut while we were there rapping: he was reaching out for me as personally as he would reach out for me impersonally during a ball game when he'd get on the bullpen phone and say: "Get McGraw ready."

Sometimes my actions embarrass me, but my feelings don't. And, thinking back on that miserable spring, the best way I know to remember my feelings is to quote myself. A few days after Gil Hodges and I talked things over, I sat down and wrote one of my diary memos, and it describes my state of mind better than I could do it now from this distance:

> I guess it could be said that I am going through a stage in my life that is nearly impossible for me to understand. It is, I suppose, a period which all the young people (as well as a great many older) in the country (world) are going through.
>
> It begins with trying to understand myself and wanting to know what I want out of life and also what I expect of life. And before I can even come close to finding these answers, I am struggling to discover exactly how to go about answering them. If by choosing a direction, and finding a reasonable answer, how can I be sure it is the right one?
>
> Who can I believe in? I believe in God and that is all. How do I know which is the proper way to Him? I want to know the difference between right and wrong: I don't. Sometimes you think you do because you have been brought up a certain way, the way of your parents or school, church, or country. But every morning you wake up only to discover that your parents are divorced, your school is not with it and your church is struggling and, worst of all, your country is falling apart.
>
> Where have I been, what have I learned, who has taught me, where am I now and, most of all, where am I going? I mean, here on earth, in this world.
>
> I feel and believe that once these things are taken care of, the supernatural (I pray it exists) will automatically be taken care of. It seems that the things that we've been taught to

believe in aren't working. The church, the government (the system), people just are having one hell of a time making it, and man, I'm a person who is really confused.

Getting my uniform on each day is something that I've dreamed of doing ever since I first heard of Babe Ruth. To be a baseball player, wow. It's the same, I'm sure, with any other person who has achieved, to an extent, a great dream. But this great dream and all the gingerbread that was strung around it was conceived in times of peace and during times when the violence and destruction that we live in today were inconceivable. Who would ever have believed that our own National Guard would ever have to show up on our own college campuses, let alone open fire on students.

Last year when we were in the heat of divisional play-offs and the World Series, everything seemed to be great. Personal problems, world problems, or governmental problems all seemed to be overshadowed by the tension and excitement of our miracle year on the field. It was wonderful. But it was only a short time after the final out was made that the fog began to clear and I found myself back down on earth and deep into the slime of reality . . . yes, the war in Southeast Asia was still going stronger than ever, people were starving to death right here in America, wonderful old U.S.A. was becoming more and more polluted and our schools, campuses, and churches were going insane. I, as a person, in the eyes of the public should have been the happiest man in the world, but I found myself in the depths of depression and fighting insanity off with every ounce of reasoning and philosophy I could grasp from my mind and heart.

To try to understand or figure any of what is going on is nearly impossible. You have to say that compared with any other government that has been tried by modern man, ours, or democracy, seems to be the best or at least offers the most for the people. It seems that we just don't seem to be able to make it work successfully. So it must be the people that are screwed up.

Our students are rallying and demonstrating against a war and against violence, and yet they inevitably end up fighting or destroying everything that gets in their way. Again — it must be the people who are missing the boat. If they're against the system and want to break away from it, fine; but it seems that their new way has equally as many faults. Why? It would appear that the people are screwed up.

I really don't know in which direction to head or what to do. Why? Because I'm a people and I'm screwed up. I think the reason I love baseball so much is because when I come into a game in the bottom of the ninth, bases loaded, no one out and a one-run lead . . . it takes people off my mind.

11

Facing the Future in
My Willie Mays Suit

FOR TERRIFICALLY DIFFERENT REASONS, the summer of
1973 was a bad one for people who worked in Washing-
ton, Wall Street, and Shea Stadium, many of whom were
in slumps. But it was a good one for Henry Aaron, who
wasn't.

For the Mets, after spending three seasons in third
place, it was a time when things went from bad to worse.
We couldn't walk on the field without breaking a bone or
pulling a hamstring muscle, my elbow was giving me
twinges, I didn't win a game for almost five months, and
we stayed in last place for two months.

But old Henry, who was thirty-nine, started the summer with 673 home runs and needed only 42 to break
Babe Ruth's record of 714. Everybody thought he'd
need two seasons to do it. But he kept hitting them and
pretty soon it became possible that he'd pass Ruth before
the year ended. Then a lot of sportswriters went around
taking polls on the subject, and I quickly put my foot in
my mouth, in addition to all my other trouble.

The key question was what would you feel like if you

were the pitcher and Aaron came to bat needing one homer for the record?

I thought it was an interesting proposition, but not an important one. So I gave what seemed like a direct answer when they got around to me. I said that if Aaron came up to bat, I'd give him my best stuff, at the same time hoping like hell he'd hit it out of the park — so long as I was a winning pitcher. You know, as a pitcher I'd have to protect my team and my pride, and that's it. So I'd give him my best shot. He doesn't need me to give him any help, he's already hit five or six off my best stuff anyway, and I see no reason why I should start to help him now.

But as a fan, I said, I wouldn't mind seeing him break Ruth's record.

Well, the only thing that came out in the paper was the first part of the statement — that I'd give Aaron my best stuff and hope he'd hit it out. Some other guys, though, said they'd lay it right down the cock and let him know it was there. Some replied in jest, and so on.

Shortly after that, Bowie Kuhn made a big investigation of the whole thing and announced that several pitchers were going to be fined and their actions with different hitters watched because they didn't want anybody laying one in there to Henry Aaron. Kuhn made a big to-do about all the replies that the guys had given. He also said he'd take "disciplinary action." And he sent telegrams to all the general managers, telling them to warn their pitchers and to read his pronouncement to them.

I knew I was on the list of the "talking" pitchers, but I wasn't notified personally. Just sat there while the commissioner was making waves and while the Mets were making only tiny ripples on the surface of the summer. So I waited two weeks, then finally wrote him a letter.

In it, I said that I was sorry he'd misunderstood what I'd told the papers and didn't think my statement was out of line in any way, shape, or form. I said I thought I'd covered myself very well by saying I'd give Henry my best stuff. But I also repeated that I hoped like hell he'd hit it out. I still stand on it as a fan, Mr. Commissioner, I wrote. And, with the respect I have for Henry Aaron, I hope he does break the record.

I'm afraid I came up cold turkey. The commissioner wrote back saying he was happy I'd written, but *unhappy* that I said I hoped he'd hit it out. He didn't like it for the integrity of the game.

Okay, I was on a losing streak, even with the commissioner of baseball. But I still don't think he understands that you can be a player and a fan simultaneously. So the problem wasn't resolved. He wasn't happy with me and I wasn't happy with him. And Henry figured to break the record long before he played against the Mets in 1974. But if I were to end up giving him a home run this year, I suppose the commissioner would end up giving me a big investigation.

The important thing, though, is that Henry Aaron will know I didn't do it intentionally. He knows I have to battle him every inch of the way. And as long as Henry knows and I know, that's all that counts.

It was like the time last August when we were the doormats of the National League's Eastern Division and the papers and fans were doing a pretty good job on us. Yogi Berra never took any courses in child psychology, that's for sure, but I remember one thing he did that wasn't too dumb. He got hold of a clipping that said the Mets were horseshit and were just going through the motions, and he came around to each player and held it up and said: "See, you're only going through the motions."

You probably think Yogi just wanted to get us riled-up. But I think it went deeper than that. It was more like my feeling about Aaron: People may have thought we were going through the motions, but they couldn't look inside our heads any more than they could look inside our locker rooms. And Yogi wanted us to realize that he didn't feel that way. He knew we'd been hurt and even crippled all summer long, but he also knew that we had enough pride left to live down the gossip — and that was all that counted.

It was completely different from 1969, when we had nothing to lose and consequently had little pressure on us. This time, the pressure was magnified a hundred times. In '69 we had a young club, and we'd never won anything before in our big-league careers. We'd been in the cellar nearly every year, and to the public we were cellar-dwellers.

So when Gil Hodges predicted that eighty-five victories would win the division championship, we weren't even thinking it might apply to us. We weren't fighting for the pennant, we were fighting for our jobs, for survival in our league. Hell, in August that year we were still thirteen games out. They buried us. But all of a sudden, we got hot and started winning, and I don't think anybody knew why we did. We used to be mathematically eliminated by August most years. But that summer there was no pressure on us, and we'd suddenly win five or six, lose one, and then win five or six more. We just took off.

In the middle of September, we'd caught up with everybody, and we stayed hot and won the division by eight games. The season was over before we even knew what the hell had happened. Then the momentum carried us through the play-off and Series. We turned out to be goddamned amazing, all right.

But in '73, it was a whole new ball game. We were expected to do well and then had a lot of injuries and collapsed. At first, I remember we'd come to the park every day and everything was cheerful, the guys were doping around, and everybody was anxious for the warm weather to come. Especially with our field — in Shea, you wait for the rain to stop and the warm weather to come because the field stays soggy. So we were looking for hot weather — and we got injuries instead.

They didn't seem too out of the ordinary for a while. But they kept piling up. In Pittsburgh that day in May, we got three guys winged by pitched balls. Then Milner pulled a hamstring. Jones hurt his wrist. The guys were starting to mumble things like "We don't need this shit" when Matlack took the line drive against his skull.

I can still see that one. I was sitting down in the bullpen watching the game on the TV monitor they keep there, the game was moving along like any other one, and the next thing you know Marty Perez of Atlanta hit a shot back at the pitcher. It happened so fast we couldn't believe it. The guys were asking, did he get his glove on the ball enough to slow it down?

Then we looked up from the TV screen and saw everybody running out to the mound, with Yogi leading the way. Jon was lying there on the ground. At that point, you just hope he's alive, it was that scary. But Jon came back ten days later and pitched okay, and just then a whole slew of other guys got hurt. We were dropping like flies.

The guys began to get conscious of injuries. You come to the park wondering who's going to be next. And sure enough, it happens. On the way back from the Coast the first week in June, we stopped in Cincinnati for two night games, two miserable rainy night games. The first night, Harrelson tried to brace himself on the ground with his hand when Bill Plummer came barreling into second, and broke his hand. The next night, we got three runs in the top of the tenth when Duffy Dyer hit a triple with the bases loaded, and we thought we had finally pulled one out. Then I gave up a walk, a single to Pete Rose, there was an error by Staub, I heaved a wild pitch, and I ended up by walking Joe Morgan.

I was being real careful with him because I didn't want him to knock in the tying run; Johnny Bench was next. So after I got too careful and walked Morgan, Yogi came out and got me. I was really pissed off. I was still grousing on the bench when Phil Hennigan came in and threw one that Bench hit over the fence for the ball game.

That screw-up may have set the stage for some negative thinking on the ball club. Some of us were getting down on Yogi for things he did. You know, I blamed him for taking me out too soon in Cincinnati — after a single, a wild pitch, and two walks. Then more injuries came, our luck kept getting worse, and the guys started griping a bit.

Finally, the newspapers got around to noticing that the Yankees were going great while the Mets were going horseshit, and they started taking surveys of their readers about who should be fired first: Yogi, Scheffing, or Don Grant. It was sick humor but, what the hell, we were sick. The polls maybe even loosened us up a little, because now we were able to joke a little more openly about Yogi instead of keeping it in whispers. Once, after the who-goes-first poll, I got smart in the clubhouse and said I wondered who'd get fired first that summer, Yogi or President Nixon? I didn't mean it too seriously, but things were going bad for both the country and the Mets at the time. But it turned out that the first to go was Spiro Agnew.

My locker was on the far side of the clubhouse in a corner at right angles to Milner, Mays, and Harry Parker. You never heard anything from Willie about Yogi, I'll say that. But everybody seemed to build up his own problem in his own mind. Like Parker, who was a math major in college and is the kind of guy who likes to have a theory or a formula for everything. He had a great arm, but there's a hell of a difference between having an equation in your head and going out and making it pitch the ball. I'd sit there and watch Harry reduce everything to a math problem and then wonder if he could make it work physically in the ninth inning.

Tom Seaver used to get a bad rap from people who thought he was too cool for words. But he wasn't. In the clubhouse he was more like a fraternity type, very mature sometimes and very Joe College other times. Then he got a reputation as a guy who couldn't pitch the "big game" under pressure. But, man, he pitches 300 innings every year without many runs to work with, and every time he throws the ball it's a pressure pitch. Just watch him when he walks on the mound — he's all concentration, always at a maximum point, always geared toward perfection, terrific on the fundamentals of pitching, and has a strong body to go with it.

I used to be kind of awed by Seaver. And once, maybe it was in 1969, my wife and I went out with him and his wife Nancy for the first time. I invited him to a Mexican restaurant we knew in Manhattan, one that didn't take reservations it was so "in." We drove up to the place and I'm thinking what a goddamned privilege it was to be double-dating with the Seavers and all, and bragging about this great restaurant — and the place was closed. Seaver laughed like hell, then took *us* to a Mexican restaurant that he knew, and we had a great time. Oh well, like I said, he's a nut for fundamentals.

Anyway, 1973 was completely different from 1969, and it had nothing to do with me and my closed restaurants. What happened was that we started to tell ourselves that we were better than sixth place, better than fifth place, better than all this criticism and flak we were taking. We weren't young anymore, we were more mature than we'd been four years earlier, we knew more about ourselves, and we knew that we hadn't even had a hot streak all summer, injuries or no injuries.

When you're new at all this and don't know what you're capable of, the way we were in '69, you discover new ways of doing things and new talents. But when you get older and people expect you to do okay, then you have to force yourself out of a slump and figure out ways of not "going through the motions." You have to *search*. What I mean is that it's harder to stay on top than it is to get there.

So that's the way things stood when we started to get

into ourselves with motivation and "you gotta believe" and all that. It sort of took hold. One day three nuns I knew, Met fans who'd been coming to Shea for years, stood up all of a sudden and uncorked this long banner that said: "YOU GOTTA BELIEVE."

By September, it became like a war cry. We started to build up a positive pressure, telling ourselves we gotta get going, gotta get going, gotta believe we can bail out. We knew we were basically a good club, and we tried to figure things out. We began to get healthy again and to work harder, and we would even play with minor injuries instead of going on sick call.

We had a terrific blend of rookies and veterans, too. I remember that we went through three catchers and then called up Ron Hodges from Memphis. We needed help so badly that we promoted him from Double-A ball to the big leagues without even trying him at Triple-A. But I remember four times he made big pinch hits that kept us in games after we started to put it together. Ken Boswell didn't play much because we had Felix Millan at second base, but Bozzie came up with one unbelievable pinch hit after another, right on through the play-off and Series. When we needed a shot the most, Krane and Jones came up with their hottest streaks of the whole season in September. Grote got so hot it was ridiculous; he could hit line drives even when he was making out, and he'd missed two months with a broken wrist. And Staub, even with two bad hands, was the big man. Maybe he can't run; it takes a triple or home run to score him from first base. But he sure as hell can play.

Then there was Harrelson, all recovered from his broken hand, Mighty Mouse playing shortstop. A super picket shortstop with a great memory. I mean, when I'm pitching badly, he'll tell me what I'm doing differently — and wrong. He'll also kick you in the ass, literally, sometimes.

Anyway, there we were in the play-offs finally, and one of my lasting memories of them was Harrelson scuffling around with Pete Rose while 50,000 people were going crazy in Shea.

We were sitting in the bullpen watching the game, with the TV monitor going full-blast. It was a superexciting kind of day because we had finally made it after that stampede in September, and we were all alert and involved when Rose went into second base.

The camera showed something going on, but you really couldn't tell what. I looked up and saw something happening on the field, about a hundred yards away. I went to the bullpen gate and forced it open and started running in toward the infield. I could see a fight was going on but didn't know who was involved. I had an idea it was between Rose and Harrelson, but didn't know why or how it had started. But I did know Rose was bigger than Harrelson, so I just thought of breaking it up or helping out.

Usually, when you run all the way in from the bullpen, the fight is over by the time you get there. You don't rush over with the idea of getting into the fight yourself or of hurting anybody. It's more of an ego thing to run there with everyone else. You know, after the fight's over, people ask, where were you during the fight? You can hardly answer, if you've just been watching it in the bullpen on the TV monitor.

Anyway, I grabbed hold of Rose and tried to pull him

off Buddy, and Alex Grammas, the Cincinnati coach, was holding onto Harrelson, and Ray Sadecki was holding onto Rose. They were pretty upset with each other. But finally we ripped them apart and the hassle seemed over.

But the next thing you know, out of the corner of your eye you see *their* bullpen guys running in. And Pedro Borbon came tearing in and broadsided Buzz Capra with a shot out of left field that you wouldn't believe. He threw it from out of nowhere right across the top of the cheekbone. Dyer saw what was going on, even though Capra didn't, and he charged over and cold-cocked Borbon and knocked him down. Then everybody started to hassle all over again.

Finally, Pedro got back up, but he must've been dizzy from the punch because he picked up a hat, or somebody handed it to him as everybody started to leave the field. But it was a Mets cap, and when he realized it, he went into a real rage.

He stuffed the cap in his mouth, with his eyes all like fire, and started to tear it apart with his teeth. Then he flung it on the ground and stomped off the field, embarrassed that he'd been caught off his guard and had slapped a Mets cap on his head in front of 50,000 people.

I don't know who won the fight, but I do know that we won the play-off after another brawl that the fans caused when some of them started to heave things at Pete in left field. Pete heaved a few things back at them. But when some guy threw out a whiskey bottle that just missed his head, Pete decided that was all for today, baby, and came trotting in toward the dugout. Then Sparky Anderson took all his guys off the field. It looked like a real bad scene because things were getting out of hand. Finally,

Chub Feeney, the president of the league, came down to our dugout and said we might have to forfeit the game if we couldn't restore order. So Yogi and a bunch of our senior citizens like Willie Mays and Seaver and Staub walked out into left field and held up their hands, pleading with the people to quit.

It was a fantastic thing, and none of us blamed the Reds for taking shelter in the dugout until things quieted down. Even after we won the play-off two days later, most of us had to run for our lives through the mob that took over the field and started to rip up the ball park.

When we flew to San Francisco two days later to open the World Series, we still felt punchy because so many hellish things had happened to us in the last six months. We'd been denounced, damned, cheered, mobbed, written off, written up, screwed up, and we were bombed out of our minds.

During this time, people were mailing us all sorts of get-well cards, good-luck charms, and voodoo dolls. Jane Jarvis, the girl who plays a storm on the organ at Shea, kept switching the music trying to help us switch our luck. A nun named Sister Kathleen sent us goodies like a baseball with a face and a pigtail. And at the height of it all, Phyllis gave birth to Cari Lynn McGraw, our second child, on September 1.

You hear so much about Charlie Finley being flamboyant that when we got to Oakland for a workout the day before the Series opened, we couldn't understand why he hadn't dressed the park up. No streamers, no bunting, no red-white-and-blue flags. It looked like the A's were getting ready for a regular-season game. Maybe he didn't want people to heist the draperies.

When the Series started the next day, sure enough, there were still no streamers or flags, and we were disappointed. The Mets had a lot of guys from the Bay area, me and Hahn and Seaver and Harrelson and Willie, and we thought our club was sure to be a good draw out there. The papers were calling it the "folk Series" between two of the more down-to-earth clubs in baseball, with lots of characters and drama on both sides. But they still didn't fill the stadium.

By contrast, for the whole previous month, it was like you were pitching in a World Series day after day. But we showed up there bracing ourselves for one last shove at the end of 180 days of almost solid playing, and we had a meeting before the game out in the empty right-field box seats. Yogi and the coaches went over all the scouting reports on their club and on *ours,* too. Our scouts had found out their report on me, because we had leaks from their side the way they did from ours. It was: look for the screwball. But I didn't think that was top-secret stuff after throwing it for eight years.

Well, I got into five of the seven games, and they were lulus. I got into the first one in the seventh inning with Oakland in front of Matlack, 2 to 1, and I pitched to eight batters the last two times around and didn't get hurt. It was my first appearance ever in a World Series and it was the day my mind kept switching from a blank to a blur of everything and everyone. I kept them from getting more runs, but they won anyway.

The next day, Koosman wasn't at his best so I got into the game in the sixth. In fact, nobody was at his best, because we'd already used Sadecki and Parker by the time I made it. I guess I wasn't at my best either. We got four runs in the top of the sixth for a lead of 6 to 3, but I started to waste it in the seventh. I hit Bert Campaneris with a pitch, walked Joe Rudi, and then Reggie Jackson doubled.

But I was still ahead, 6 to 4, when they went to the bottom of the ninth. But I made one major mistake that a relief pitcher is never supposed to make: No matter how big a lead you've got, you've still got to get the side out. So Deron Johnson pinch-hit a double, then I got two guys out, but I walked Sal Bando and got raked for singles by Jackson and Gene Tenace, and it was tied at six-all.

By the time we got four more in the twelfth and won it, a lot of crazy things happened. I wound up pitching six innings, Willie had trouble with two fly balls in the sun, Mike Andrews made two errors at second base for the A's, and Augie Donatelli blew a call at the plate. I know he blew it because he slipped and was lying on the ground when Bud Harrelson tried to score on a fly to left by Felix Millan, and Rudi threw him out at home. I mean, Augie ruled that he threw Bud out at home, but I thought he was sort of guessing that the ball beat the runner there. Willie thought Augie missed it, too, because he was on deck at the time watching. He got down on his hands and knees alongside Donatelli like he was praying or something and squealed, "How can you call the man out, how can you do it?"

Anyway, even after we got all those runs in the twelfth, we still weren't safe. Jackson hit a triple off me in the bottom of the inning: In three straight times up, he had really worn me out with a single, double, and triple. This time, the ball fell in because the sun got in Willie's eyes. Then when I walked Tenace, there was Yogi out of the dugout asking me, "Are you tired?" I'd worked eight innings in two days and I said, "I guess I am." So he brought in George Stone and I sat and watched Stone sweat it out. He did, too. Jesus Alou hit a single for one run right away, but Stone finally got them out and McGraw had his first win in a World Series.

The Series turned out to be a pretty wacky show, from start to finish. We'd lost the first game on a ball that went through Felix's legs at second base, and they lost the second on a pair of boots by Mike Andrews at second base. Then we had three games in New York that resembled little riots, with something like 160,000 people jamming the park on three ice-cold nights and all sorts of hell breaking out behind the scenes, most of it between Finley and his players.

I'll tell you, Mike Andrews is as human as anybody else, so we felt sorry for him when Finley tried to railroad him home with a medical letter saying that Mike agreed he wasn't able to play anymore. We thought the Oakland players were exceptional guys, damned fine ballplayers and real loose all the time. And you ask, how can a guy who owns a ball club and deals with athletes all those years do a thing like that — how can he rationalize it? You almost think there must be a different reason than the public one: guy drops ground ball, guy throws wild to first base, owner gets pissed off, owner dumps him.

When Andrews finally was brought back a few days later in New York, after the A's and the commissioner wouldn't go along with it, he got a terrific ovation — even after he grounded out to Garrett. You really felt great for the guy when he went back to their dugout, with everybody standing up and cheering like mad, and even our bench felt like applauding.

The McGraw family had a little run-in with Mr. Finley's system, too, and I nearly blew my stack. Phyllis and Lynn Dyer were stopped at the turnstile going into the Oakland ball park before the sixth game because they were carrying my son Mark: the guard said they'd have to have a ticket for Mark, even though he was eighteen months old and was going to sit on Phyl's lap. Checkpoint Charlie, my ass.

They finally telephoned the dugout and I came hustling out there in my uniform to see what the hell was going on. The guard kept changing his tune, kept coming up with new "rules" that he said Mr. Finley made them enforce at the gate. He and I even got into a shoving match and I was getting set to knock him on his tail when somebody else from the Mets staff came up and got them through. The next day, the guard apologized and said he was under orders. Everybody out there was too scared to make decisions like that on their own.

But for the entire Oakland team, stuff like that going on behind the scenes in foul territory seemed to bring out the best in them. Between the foul lines, they were super players. And if I got any "answers" to the questions rattling around in my head at the time, it was probably from realizing that a lot of other people besides McGraw have monkeys on their backs and are trying to find out *why*. I think we all understood each other.

One day they wrote in the paper that Dick Green said "that guy, what's-his-name, has a good screwball." The next day, I went up to him and stuck out my hand and said, "Hello, I'm what's-his-name." Green laughed and said, "Look, man, I wasn't trying to rip you or anything," and we both sort of laughed it off.

Another time I walked Tenace on a three-and-two screwball, and when he was standing on first base I looked over and said, "How can you take that pitch, man?" He's a good cat, too. I like to call him "Tenatchee," because it sounds so much better for a baseball player than "Tennis." He just pointed to his eyes, like saying: "Great eyes, man, great eyes." Then he made third on a long fly ball as the inning ended and I called over: "Hey, man, how did you get over there that fast?" And he pointed to his legs and said: "Got to have good wheels, too, man."

When Deron Johnson got that pinch-hit double off me in the second game, I met him the next day on the field and said: "That's not too neighborly, man." He owns a ranch house down the hill from me near San Diego, and I told him: "When you were with the Phillies, I used to walk you every time." And Deron said: "Look, I've been playing fourteen years and this is the first World Series I've ever been in." He said it kind of apologetically, too, so I said: "In that case, neighbor, go ahead and rip."

What I mean is that they were reasonable guys, and maybe that's the real message when you start to analyze yourself or other ballplayers or anybody, for that matter. Finley abused Mike Andrews as a person because Andrews had screwed up something as a player. That's horseshit, and it misses the point. You don't have to play, or even pay, a guy if he can't cut it as a player; but you've got to feel for him if he's trying to cut it as a person.

The only ruckus we had on the Mets during the

Series was in the sixth and seventh games, which we lost just when we had the jump on Oakland, three games to two, and needed only one more to win the Series. Some of the guys wondered why we pitched Seaver in the sixth game and Matlack in the seventh. They felt Seaver was tired and could've been held back a day, and maybe Stone should've started the sixth game instead. He'd pitched super all season and deserved the shot. But Yogi went with Seaver, and the club stopped hitting, anyway.

But we didn't go to pieces and start running around trying to blame people, not after all that we had gone through, and not after what the Oakland players had gone through. We all learned something from living in the same pressure cooker for so long.

I guess I learned as much from Willie Mays as anybody, and maybe it'll settle me down into a better guy, maybe even a better pitcher.

You know, Willie was forty-two and he was hurt a lot. He got down on himself after a while because he knew he was going to retire and he wanted to help the club and also not embarrass himself. Sometimes he forced himself to play, and then he'd get hurt again while trying to do it. He also knew that Yogi was taking a lot of guff, and he didn't want to get involved in making things worse.

So he didn't go around second-guessing anybody in the clubhouse, and on the bus and plane he really made himself fit in. I mean, he was with us only two years and he was twice as old as some of the guys, but you'd think he'd spent his whole twenty years in the bigs with them.

When we were flying to Oakland for the Series, me and Krane and Koos and Willie were playing hearts in the back of the plane. Willie got up to get a Coke or something and caught the seat of his pants on the ashtray on the arm of the chair. It made a little snag in his pants, and he started whining: "Damn, now I gotta fix my pants, I got a hole in them. Guess I'll just get rid of 'em."

"Damn it, Willie, they're good pants," I said, making sure McGraw would be heard from. "All they've got is a hole in them. Why don't you get them fixed and wear them?" But he said, "Man, no, can't wear them this way." So I said: "If you're not going to wear them, they look like they'll fit me. Put 'em in my locker."

He came back and said, "Try on my coat." Fairly perfect. "Man," he said, "that looks good on you. But the pants got a hole in them, and you don't want to wear 'em that way."

"Willie," I said, "there's no hole in your pants that's too big for me to wear."

A few days later, there was the suit in my locker. The whole suit. Doubleknit, blue and white, a good-looking print, quality stuff, and it fit me like it was tailor-made. Now I call it my Willie Mays suit.

Willie started life with nothing and wound up earning everything, and he has a lot of fun now realizing how much he busted his ass to get it. Now people take good care of him, he gets deals on things, so he tries to share his life. He likes his privacy, but that's human. And I know he and Yogi had a tough time as far as the line-up went, and a lot of times maybe Willie didn't want to come to the park at all — so as not to cause trouble about whether he should be in the line-up. He was even afraid his "retirement night" might disrupt the club when it was going good at the end.

Anyway, when we flew home from Oakland after the

first weekend there, I learned pretty much the same thing from some people who live near us. We live in a cul-de-sac in Manhasset on Long Island in the summer, but we don't really know our neighbors. They commute, and we go back to California in the fall, and we never really get together. But this time, the Mets had somehow gone through all that misery and won the Eastern championship and the pennant, and now we were all even in the World Series, one game apiece.

We drove from the airport to Manhasset and up to the cul-de-sac, and suddenly all the neighbors came out, even though it was late at night, and we didn't even know if they were baseball fans or anything. But there they came, and there up on the house they'd strung this big white bed sheet that they'd painted, and all it said in big letters was: "We Believe."

A few days later, it was the seventh game of the Series and we were back in Oakland. Ninth inning, the A's had us, 5 to 1, and we had only three outs to go in the whole unbelievable season. Yogi called down: "Get McGraw ready." So I started throwing on the grass in the bullpen down the right-field line.

Reggie Jackson came out to take his position for the last time in 1973, unless we got hot and scored four big ones. I remembered that he'd been quoted as saying he hoped the Reds would get in the Series because they had stars and he hadn't heard about anybody on our club. But I couldn't believe Reggie Jackson would say that, so I didn't take it too literally, especially not after some of the good things he said about Mike Andrews and some other issues. I was getting some good vibes from him, anyway.

While I was warming up, he called over and said:

"Tug, don't bother warming up, we got you now. You might've had an edge on us before, but we got you now." Then Milner walked, Hahn singled, and, with two down, Krane pinch-hit a grounder that Tenace booted behind first base. Now it was 5 to 2, and the amazing Mets were stirring around, and I was warming up faster now. And I shouted over to him: "Hey, Reggie, we're going to get *you* now."

And Reggie kind of took a breath. He didn't exactly say "You gotta believe" or anything like that. But he sort of conceded the point that a lot of us had started to believe, and he called over: "You might, at that."

But then Garrett popped a little fly behind shortstop that Campaneris caught in his cradle and it was over. I quit throwing and headed for the dugout while all hell broke loose, and I looked around for Reggie Jackson. But by then he had disappeared in the crowd.

When it's over, you realize how tired you really are, and you sit in the locker room and say, It was a bummer to lose, but I'm really glad it's over. I can't wait to get home and put it all behind me for a while. One day you grow up, and you're just what you are when you get there. Me and my screwball, and my doubleknit, blue-and-white Willie Mays suit.